Reading Improvement

Exercises

for Students

of English

as a Second Language

PRENTICE-HALL INTERNATIONAL, INC., *London*
PRENTICE-HALL OF AUSTRALIA, PTY., LTD., *Sydney*
PRENTICE-HALL OF CANADA, LTD., *Toronto*
PRENTICE-HALL OF INDIA (PRIVATE) LTD., *New Delhi*
PRENTICE-HALL OF JAPAN, INC., *Tokyo*

Reading Improvement

Exercises

DAVID P. HARRIS

Director, American Language Institute
Associate Professor of English
Georgetown University

for Students

of English

as a Second Language

Prentice-Hall, Inc., Englewood Cliffs, New Jersey

Current printing (last digit):
11

© 1966 by Prentice-Hall, Inc., Englewood Cliffs, N.J.

Library of Congress Catalog Card No.: 66-10380

Printed in the United States of America [75505-C]

Preface

These exercises are designed for high-intermediate and advanced learners of English as a second language who need practice in improving their reading speed and comprehension in order to perform effectively in colleges and universities where English is the language of instruction and where, perhaps, they must compete with students whose native language is English. It has been our experience that even "advanced" learners of English as a second language tend to be slow readers, and that their slow reading speed constitutes a serious handicap when they commence their studies at our universities. Therefore the emphasis in these exercises is on *increasing reading speed,* not on vocabulary development as such. Reading materials have been selected for their appropriateness for college students, though they have usually been simplified somewhat, as required for speed-reading exercises. All the exercises in the book have been tested on substantial numbers of higher-level learners of English as a second language.

GENERAL PLAN OF THE BOOK

The book is divided into five parts, which should be taken up in sequence for maximum effectiveness. Part I consists of a set of diagnostic tests to determine the students' general reading competence at the outset of the program. Parts II through VII are designed to provide practice in responding rapidly but accurately to increasingly longer units of writing: first the word, then the sentence, the paragraph, and finally the complete composition. Part VIII deals with the techniques of scanning for particular information. Part IX is comprised of two exercises on the use of the dictionary, the emphasis again being on increasing speed of response. All exercises are to be timed so that two scores are obtained: one for speed and the other for accuracy. A key to the exercises and a reading-time conversion table for those exercises involving longer reading selections are provided at the back of the book.

PROCEDURE FOR CONDUCTING THE EXERCISES

The instructor should first go over the directions with the class, making certain that this material is understood by all the students. Then the class should be started on the exercise together, the instructor keeping the time. As each student completes the exercise, his time should be recorded. (See below for suggestions on timing the exercises.) When all the students have finished the exercise, they should score their work, using the key at the back of the book. Finally, opportunity should be given for discussion of the students' problems.

TIMING THE EXERCISES

For timing the exercises, the instructor should have either a stop watch or a clock or watch with a second hand.

If the class is small, the instructor may wish to record the students' times himself by having the students raise their hands immediately upon completion of the exercise. These times can later be transferred to the students' books when everyone has finished.

If the class is too large to permit the instructor's keeping the record of the students' times, the following method is recommended.
1. Before beginning the exercise, the instructor writes the following on the blackboard:

MIN.	SEC.
0	0
	15
	30
	45

2. The instructor starts the class together, carefully noting the starting time.
3. As the students work the exercise, the instructor writes the number of completed minutes under the MIN. column and points to the quarter-minutes in the SEC. column.
4. Immediately upon completing the exercise, each student writes his time on the space provided after the exercise, recording both minutes and quarter-minutes: 4/15, 6/45, 8/0.

vi

INSTRUCTOR'S GUIDE

To help instructors to interpret their students' performance on the exercises, an *Instructor's Guide* will be made available from the publisher upon request. This Guide provides data on the performance both of advanced-level students of English as a second language and also of American college freshmen.

ACKNOWLEDGMENTS

In selecting types of exercises for this book, the writer consulted many excellent reading-improvement texts for native speakers of English, borrowing those devices which seemed particularly appropriate for the instruction of students of English as a second language. To the authors of these books—too numerous to mention individually—he wishes to acknowledge his great indebtedness. Thanks are due also to the many teachers who volunteered to test the materials in their classes, most notable being the staff of the American Language Institute of Georgetown University. Finally, he wishes to express his deep gratitude to Miss Lois McArdle of the Program for the Testing of English as a Foreign Language for her very considerable assistance in preparing the materials for publication.

D. P. H.

Contents

PART ONE Diagnosing Your Reading Ability

Exercise 1: Diagnostic Vocabulary Test   3
Exercise 2: Diagnostic Reading Test   11

PART TWO Increasing Your Word-Recognition Speed

Exercise 3: Word Recognition   23
Exercise 4: Word Recognition — Continued   27
Exercise 5: Word-Pair Recognition   31

PART THREE Increasing Your Word-Comprehension Speed

Exercise 6: Word Comprehension   37
Exercise 7: Sames and Opposites   39

PART FOUR Increasing Your Sentence-Comprehension Speed

Exercise 8: Sentence Completion   43
Exercise 9: Reading Sentences for General Meaning   49

PART FIVE Reading Paragraphs for Central Idea

Exercise 10: Reading for Central Idea   55

PART SIX Reading Paragraphs for Full Understanding

Exercise 11: Paragraph Comprehension   79

PART SEVEN Reading the Whole Composition

Exercise 12: Noah Webster   103
Exercise 13: Professor Agassiz and the Fish   109
Exercise 14: Scandinavian Influence on the English Vocabulary   115

PART EIGHT Reading to Locate Specific Information: Scanning

Exercise 15: Scanning Short Paragraphs   123
Exercise 16: Scanning an Article   145

PART NINE Using the Dictionary

Exercise 17: Finding Information in the Dictionary   159
Exercise 18: "Catchwords"   165

Key to the Exercises   171

Reading-Time Conversion Table for Exercises 2, 12, 13, 14   177

Reading Improvement Exercises for Students of English as a Second Language

PART ONE

Diagnosing Your Reading Ability

Before you begin this series of reading-improvement exercises, it would be useful for you to find out how well you now read English. The two exercises in this section are designed to test both your reading speed and your comprehension.

The first of these exercises is a Diagnostic Vocabulary Test made up of relatively easy English words. When this test was given to college freshmen who were native speakers of English, it was found that most students took no more than six or seven minutes to complete the 65 problems, and made no more than one or two errors. If you have much difficulty with these problems, you probably still lack a good "working vocabulary" for dealing with college-level reading materials. The exercises in this book do not concentrate on vocabulary building; you will have to work on this problem yourself, primarily by doing as much reading as you can.

The second of the exercises is a Reading Comprehension Test, consisting of a 1000-word essay followed by a series of questions about the content of the essay. By timing your reading of the selection, you can determine the speed at which you can read college materials of moderate difficulty. Your score on the comprehension questions will give you some idea of how well you can understand what you read. And, incidentally, you should find the reading selection interesting in itself, for it offers sound advice on increasing your vocabulary.

1

Diagnosing Your Reading Ability

Name _____

Diagnostic Vocabulary Test

Directions: Each problem consists of a test word followed by four possible definitions. Put a check mark on the line before the best definition of the test word.

Example:

wealthy

_____ (a) dry

_____ (b) strong

___✓___ (c) rich

_____ (d) sad

Work as rapidly and as accurately as you can. You will probably find most of the test words quite easy. But try to answer every problem, even if you are not sure your answer is correct.

Be sure to time yourself on the test. As soon as you finish, record your time on the line marked TIME just after the last problem.

1. tiny

_____ (a) very swift

_____ (b) very strong

_____ (c) very small

_____ (d) very sharp

2. sketch

_____ (a) a long, deep cut

_____ (b) a loud, warning cry

_____ (c) a simple, rough drawing

_____ (d) a small, light boat

3. moist

_____ (a) slightly wet

_____ (b) quite large

_____ (c) very dark

_____ (d) rather noisy

4. nap

_____ (a) a happy song

_____ (b) a short meeting

_____ (c) a sharp rock

_____ (d) a brief sleep

5. ache

_____ (a) a dull pain

_____ (b) a sharp knife

_____ (c) a sudden thought

_____ (d) a deep cut

6. glance

_____ (a) a loud cry

_____ (b) a brief look

_____ (c) a quick reply

_____ (d) a sharp weapon

7. astonish
_____ (a) to destroy entirely
_____ (b) to hide completely
_____ (c) to shout loudly
_____ (d) to surprise suddenly

8. gigantic
_____ (a) excited
_____ (b) foolish
_____ (c) huge
_____ (d) dangerous

9. swamp
_____ (a) a piece of soft, wet land
_____ (b) a kind of strong, thick rope
_____ (c) a group of small, low houses
_____ (d) a flash of clear, bright light

10. chilly
_____ (a) quite foolish
_____ (b) extremely rough
_____ (c) rather cold
_____ (d) very sick

11. brass
_____ (a) a rough cloth
_____ (b) a yellow metal
_____ (c) a thick plant
_____ (d) a farm animal

12. vanish
_____ (a) to paint
_____ (b) to disappear
_____ (c) to defeat
_____ (d) to suffer

13. pond
_____ (a) a small body of water
_____ (b) a large pile of earth
_____ (c) a strong wall of stone
_____ (d) a thick mass of trees

14. console
_____ (a) to save
_____ (b) to correct
_____ (c) to examine
_____ (d) to comfort

15. feeble
_____ (a) false
_____ (b) weak
_____ (c) dark
_____ (d) silent

16. gaze
_____ (a) to burn brightly
_____ (b) to sleep briefly
_____ (c) to walk slowly
_____ (d) to look steadily

17. hazard
_____ (a) a danger
_____ (b) a storm
_____ (c) a battle
_____ (d) a fire

4

18. fragrant
   _____ (a) sweet-smelling
   _____ (b) fast-moving
   _____ (c) finely built
   _____ (d) easily broken

19. chat
   _____ (a) an untruthful story
   _____ (b) a friendly greeting
   _____ (c) an informal talk
   _____ (d) a noisy quarrel

20. stare
   _____ (a) to speak in anger
   _____ (b) to move in a circle
   _____ (c) to climb with difficulty
   _____ (d) to look long and hard

21. slender
   _____ (a) long and thin
   _____ (b) polite and kind
   _____ (c) complete and final
   _____ (d) hard and strong

22. dismiss
   _____ (a) to look for
   _____ (b) to send away
   _____ (c) to pour out
   _____ (d) to cut apart

23. keen
   _____ (a) brief
   _____ (b) ugly
   _____ (c) new
   _____ (d) sharp

24. handy
   _____ (a) attractive
   _____ (b) powerful
   _____ (c) convenient
   _____ (d) careful

25. mend
   _____ (a) to repair
   _____ (b) to remember
   _____ (c) to report
   _____ (d) to return

26. drowsy
   _____ (a) hungry
   _____ (b) friendly
   _____ (c) ugly
   _____ (d) sleepy

27. tumble
   _____ (a) to talk quietly
   _____ (b) to walk slowly
   _____ (c) to fall suddenly
   _____ (d) to strike repeatedly

28. trivial
   _____ (a) difficult to believe
   _____ (b) of little importance
   _____ (c) lacking good sense
   _____ (d) strange in appearance

5

29. spade

———— (a) a tool for digging

———— (b) a large, flat field

———— (c) a device for writing

———— (d) a long, deep valley

30. reckless

———— (a) useless

———— (b) hopeless

———— (c) careless

———— (d) worthless

31. mute

———— (a) hungry

———— (b) angry

———— (c) little

———— (d) silent

32. discard

———— (a) to oppose

———— (b) to throw away

———— (c) to injure

———— (d) to find by accident

33. pebble

———— (a) a wide stream

———— (b) a high hill

———— (c) a deep hole

———— (d) a small stone

34. weary

———— (a) early

———— (b) careful

———— (c) tired

———— (d) unhappy

35. conceal

———— (a) to describe

———— (b) to injure

———— (c) to praise

———— (d) to hide

36. strive

———— (a) to wait very eagerly

———— (b) to measure very carefully

———— (c) to walk very rapidly

———— (d) to try very hard

37. gloomy

———— (a) foolish

———— (b) sad

———— (c) timid

———— (d) open

38. ponder

———— (a) to walk slowly

———— (b) to consider carefully

———— (c) to hold tightly

———— (d) to speak softly

39. wrath

———— (a) great anger

———— (b) a large crowd

———— (c) hard labor

———— (d) a sudden storm

40. tap

———— (a) to sleep briefly

———— (b) to strike lightly

———— (c) to tie tightly

———— (d) to run quickly

6

41. blunder
_____ (a) a sudden fall
_____ (b) a deep thought
_____ (c) a loud noise
_____ (d) a foolish mistake

42. speck
_____ (a) a small spot
_____ (b) a cruel remark
_____ (c) a strange sight
_____ (d) a short talk

43. hoist
_____ (a) to raise up
_____ (b) to shout joyfully
_____ (c) to throw away
_____ (d) to wash thoroughly

44. hurl
_____ (a) to cry with pain
_____ (b) to throw with force
_____ (c) to depart in haste
_____ (d) to injure in anger

45. yearn
_____ (a) to acquire great wealth
_____ (b) to speak at great length
_____ (c) to feel great desire
_____ (d) to cause great damage

46. twig
_____ (a) a double amount
_____ (b) a small branch
_____ (c) a sudden push
_____ (d) a sharp stone

47. haul
_____ (a) to shout
_____ (b) to cover
_____ (c) to cut
_____ (d) to pull

48. gale
_____ (a) an ancient story
_____ (b) a strong wind
_____ (c) a serious accident
_____ (d) a high wall

49. stray
_____ (a) to lift up
_____ (b) to throw away
_____ (c) to wander away
_____ (d) to burn up

50. lull
_____ (a) a soft area of land
_____ (b) a short period of quiet
_____ (c) a small group of people
_____ (d) a loud cry of pain

51. shrewd
_____ (a) clever
_____ (b) torn
_____ (c) rough
_____ (d) afraid

7

52. apparel
_____ (a) clothing
_____ (b) knowledge
_____ (c) fear
_____ (d) shelter

53. snatch
_____ (a) to break completely
_____ (b) to strike forcefully
_____ (c) to examine closely
_____ (d) to seize suddenly

54. haughty
_____ (a) old and tired
_____ (b) weak and frightened
_____ (c) proud and scornful
_____ (d) young and happy

55. dwindle
_____ (a) to burn brightly
_____ (b) to walk slowly
_____ (c) to become smaller
_____ (d) to grow angry

56. bewildered
_____ (a) greatly angered
_____ (b) greatly confused
_____ (c) greatly amused
_____ (d) greatly injured

57. bough
_____ (a) a high wall
_____ (b) a wide street
_____ (c) a loud laugh
_____ (d) a large branch

58. crave
_____ (a) to cover completely
_____ (b) to deny strongly
_____ (c) to desire greatly
_____ (d) to wash carefully

59. shun
_____ (a) to push
_____ (b) to avoid
_____ (c) to burn
_____ (d) to brighten

60. twine
_____ (a) a pleasant drink
_____ (b) great success
_____ (c) a double amount
_____ (d) strong string

61. lofty
_____ (a) very amusing
_____ (b) very frequent
_____ (c) very high
_____ (d) very expensive

62. scorch

_____ (a) to burn slightly
_____ (b) to act superior to
_____ (c) to examine carefully
_____ (d) to cut the surface of

63. kindle

_____ (a) to reduce in size
_____ (b) to set on fire
_____ (c) to handle roughly
_____ (d) to act friendly toward

64. wade

_____ (a) to observe from a distance
_____ (b) to beat with the hands
_____ (c) to walk through water
_____ (d) to tear into pieces

65. genial

_____ (a) strong and bold
_____ (b) noble and wise
_____ (c) cheerful and friendly
_____ (d) famous and respected

TIME _____

SCORE _____

9

EXERCISE 2

Diagnostic Reading Test

Directions: Read the following selection at your normal speed; try to comprehend as much as you can in one reading. Time yourself carefully, and as soon as you finish the selection, record your time on the line marked TIME after the last line of the selection. Then go on to the Reading Comprehension Quiz that follows.

In reading the selection, you will find that some of the hard words and phrases are defined in footnotes. If you already know the meaning of these words and phrases, do not take the time to read the footnotes. And if there are other words that are unfamiliar to you, do not stop to think about them, but continue your reading. Usually you will find that the rest of the sentence will make their general meaning clear to you.

Remember: try to read at your usual rate, and read for understanding.

Learning New Words

The exact number of English words is not known and cannot be known. The large ("unabridged") dictionaries have over half a million entries, but many of these are compound words (*schoolroom, sugar bowl*) or different derivatives of the same word (*rare—rarely, rarefy, rarity*), and a good many are obsolete [1] words to help us read older literature. Dictionaries do not attempt to cover completely many large groups of words that we can draw on: [2] the informal vocabulary, especially slang,[3] localisms,[4] the terms of various occupations and professions; words used only occasionally by scientists and specialists in many fields; foreign words borrowed for use in English; or many of the three thousand or more new words or new senses of words that come into use every year and that may or may not be used long enough to warrant being included. It would be conservative to say that there are over a million English words that any of us might meet in our listening and reading and that we may draw on in our speaking and writing.

The individual's vocabulary

How many words an individual uses cannot be exactly measured either, but there are numerous estimates. Professor Seashore concluded that first-graders enter school with at least 24,000 words and add 5,000 each year so that they leave high

---

[1] OBSOLETE: no longer in use.

[2] DRAW ON: make use of.

[3] SLANG: colorful or amusing language used in very informal situations.

[4] LOCALISMS: expressions used in only one part of the country.

From *Writer's Guide and Index to English* by Porter G. Perrin. Copyright © 1959 by Scott, Foresman & Company. Reprinted by permission of Scott, Foresman & Company.

school with at least 80,000. These figures are for *recognition* vocabulary, the words we understand when we read or hear them. Our *active* vocabulary, the words we use in speaking and writing, is considerably smaller.

You cannot always produce a word exactly when you want it, as you probably know from the annoying experience of trying to remember the name of a casual acquaintance. But consciously using the words you recognize in reading will help get them into your active vocabulary. Occasionally in your reading pay particular attention to these words, especially when the subject is one that you might well write or talk about. Underline or make a list of words that you feel a need for and look up the less familiar ones in a dictionary. And then before very long find a way to use some of them. Once you know how they are pronounced and what they stand for, you can safely use them.

Increasing vocabulary by learning new subjects

"But my vocabulary is so small!" is a common complaint of students in composition courses and of other people who have some intention of writing. Or they say, "I know what I mean but I can't put it into words." If your vocabulary is small, that is only the symptom [5] and not the disease, for words cannot be considered apart from their meaning and usefulness. If you have a clear idea of what you want to say, you won't have much trouble trying to find the words to express it. There are sense impressions, moods, and feelings—a variety of subjective sensations—for which you may have no specific words, but in most of your writing you are not discussing these. Not being able to "find the words" usually means not being able to think out very clearly what you want to say.

The words you already have are in the areas of your knowledge and your interest. Consequently, the most natural way to increase your stock of words is by learning something more, something new, perhaps from observation or conversation or

---

[5] SYMPTOM: a sign of a disease.

from reading a magazine or a college textbook. You can't take facts and ideas away with you unless they are in verbal form.[6] The easiest way to extend your vocabulary is by acquiring groups of words from new experience. In learning to drive a car, you picked up a number of new words; you will learn several in visiting a printing plant or a radio station or some other new place for the first time. New words come from every experience, from every job, every sport, every art, every book, from every field of thought and study. Consider the words that would be added to a person's vocabulary from a newly acquired interest in mathematics, cooking, sailing, music, poetry, or economics.

To make these new words your own, you must know what they stand for. Explain to someone what you have just learned, talk it over with somebody else who is interested in it, try to teach it to someone who knows nothing about it, or write about it.

In college your stock of facts and ideas increases enormously, with a corresponding increase in vocabulary. As you come to understand what *registrar, curriculum, schedule, major field,* stand for you will find yourself using them easily and naturally, as well as the colloquial [7] and slang vocabulary of the campus (*dorm, grad student, poly sci, math*); you may take up a new sport or some other activity and acquire more words; and a course in a new field will probably add three or four hundred new words to your vocabulary, some of them technical and of restricted use,[8] many of them of more general application. Acquiring the vocabularies of biology or sociology or history is an essential part of your courses; certainly you can't go far without the names of the facts and the ideas which are being treated.

You should learn these words accurately *the first time you meet them;* look at their spelling, pronounce them as you hear them in class or as a dictionary indicates, and study their exact meaning. Probably a good deal of students' trouble in courses

---

[6] IN VERBAL FORM: in the form of words.

[7] COLLOQUIAL . . . VOCABULARY: the words and expressions belonging to conversation and informal writing.

[8] RESTRICTED USE: limited (specialized) use.

comes from only partly understanding the specialized words when they are first met. Once these words are understood, they should be used. Many of them will be needed in class discussion or examinations or term papers, but using them in talking over the course work or using them casually in conversation will help impress on your mind what they stand for and therefore make the words themselves come more easily. In this way you will acquire those thousands of words which the studies on vocabulary credit a college graduate.

TIME _____*

---

* After you finish the rest of the exercise, consult the reading-time conversion table on pp. 177-78 to determine your *reading rate*.

Reading Comprehension Quiz

Directions: For each problem, put a check mark before the one choice (a, b, c, or d) which correctly completes the sentence or answers the question. *Do not look back at the reading selection in working these problems.*

1. About how many entries are contained in large ("unabridged") English dictionaries?
   _____ (a) almost a quarter of a million
   _____ (b) a third of a million
   _____ (c) a half million
   _____ (d) over a million

2. About how many words does the writer estimate there are in English?
   _____ (a) a half million
   _____ (b) three-quarters of a million
   _____ (c) one million
   _____ (d) two million

3. One's *recognition* vocabulary is
   _____ (a) the same thing as his *active* vocabulary
   _____ (b) less often used than his *active* vocabulary
   _____ (c) usually smaller than his *active* vocabulary
   _____ (d) much larger than his *active* vocabulary

4. The writer mentions Professor Seashore's
   _____ (a) method of learning new words
   _____ (b) estimate of how many words children know
   _____ (c) study of slang words and localisms
   _____ (d) count of the number of words in an unabridged dictionary

5. The writer does NOT suggest increasing our vocabulary by
_____ (a) underlining useful words we find in our reading
_____ (b) using new words casually in our conversation
_____ (c) trying to teach someone else something we have just learned
_____ (d) devoting half an hour each day to the study of the dictionary

6. The word *schoolroom* is used in the essay as an example of
_____ (a) a compound
_____ (b) an obsolete term
_____ (c) a derivative
_____ (d) a specialized term

7. According to the writer, the easiest way to increase our stock of words is by
_____ (a) trying to write about our sense impressions and feelings
_____ (b) making a systematic study of the dictionary
_____ (c) acquiring groups of words from new experiences
_____ (d) thinking out very clearly what we want to say

8. Why did the writer mention learning to drive a car?
_____ (a) To compare the good habits of driving with the good habits of vocabulary building.
_____ (b) As an example of an activity which becomes easier when we know the proper technical terms.
_____ (c) To show that it is as easy to learn new words as it is to drive a car.
_____ (d) As an example of an experience which causes us to pick up new words.

9. According to the writer, people who say they "can't find the words"
_____ (a) usually aren't able to think out very clearly what they want to say
_____ (b) simply haven't learned how to use the dictionary properly
_____ (c) should develop more special interests in order to increase their vocabularies
_____ (d) generally have too small an active vocabulary for their needs

10. Which of the following do the dictionaries attempt to cover most completely?
_____ (a) localisms
_____ (b) derivatives
_____ (c) slang
_____ (d) campus colloquialisms

SCORE _____

PART TWO

Increasing Your Word-Recognition Speed

The exercises in this section are designed to give you practice in responding rapidly but accurately to the appearance of English words and phrases. This ability is obviously of great importance for effective reading, for if you misread words you will soon lose the sense of what you are reading and will waste time by having to go back over the material again.

There are two very common ways in which words are misread, especially in rapid reading. First, you may confuse words that *look* similar, such as *path* and *bath,* or *band* and *bend.* This kind of mistake is particularly likely if your native language does not use an alphabet like that of English.

Second, if you have to say words to yourself when you read, you may confuse words which *sound* similar, such as *heat* and *hit, path* and *pass.* You may even have this difficulty when you read in your native language—many people do. And of course the problem is likely to be much greater when you are reading a less familiar language.

These exercises, then, may be useful to you in two ways: by giving you practice in increasing your word-recognition speed while at the same time enabling you to determine whether you make either of the common kinds of reading errors described above. If, in working the exercises, you find that you frequently confuse words which look similar, it would be wise to devote more time to the rapid reading of simple materials in English. Lists of similar-looking words would be ideal for this purpose, and perhaps your teacher can help you find suitable lists to work with. If, on the other hand, you seem to confuse words that sound similar, it is likely that these errors reflect difficulties with the pronunciation of English. Your teacher can recommend pronunciation drills directed at your specific problems.

21

Name _____

Word Recognition

Directions: Each problem consists of a "test word" followed by five other words, one of which is exactly the same as the "test word." Find which one it is and underline it.

Example: TEST WORD
| got | get | pot | hot | god | got |

In the example, the last of the five words is the same as the "test word," *got*.

Work as rapidly and as accurately as you can.

TEST WORDS					
1. home	whom	hone	hum	home	some
2. class	clasp	claps	class	close	clash
3. ship	ship	sheep	hips	shop	chip
4. least	list	lost	feast	last	least
5. cheap	chip	cheap	ship	sheep	cheat
6. break	brake	brick	break	bleak	broke
7. spot	stop	sport	pots	spot	shot
8. part	port	past	trap	dart	part
9. know	knew	no	know	now	known
10. done	dome	poem	done	bone	dune
11. saw	sew	saw	was	law	sat
12. lack	lock	luck	lark	lack	look
13. taste	toast	tossed	test	task	taste
14. moon	moan	noon	moon	none	man
15. chop	chop	shop	chap	shod	shad
16. best	bets	pest	desk	best	pets
17. deer	peer	deep	beer	deer	deed

23

18. beat	peat	deep	beet	pate	beat
19. split	spilt	spits	split	spill	slips
20. coast	cost	coast	coats	cast	cots
21. flew	slew	flaw	flew	slaw	few
22. match	watch	math	mash	much	match
23. prove	proof	drove	prow	pore	prove
24. flesh	fresh	flesh	slash	flash	left
25. seed	seat	seep	speed	seed	sees
26. beet	beat	deep	beet	peat	best
27. west	vest	west	vets	wets	wits
28. theme	theme	team	them	hem	then
29. rust	ruts	rest	lust	lest	rust
30. sore	scar	sore	sort	sole	rose
31. since	cents	sense	sins	since	scent
32. both	bath	path	doth	both	booth
33. meat	meal	meat	mate	met	neat
34. dock	pock	desk	duck	peck	dock
35. lips	laps	slip	lips	lisp	leaps
36. blew	brew	blue	blow	brow	blew
37. shall	small	shell	halls	shall	shale
38. brick	prick	drink	brick	brisk	brink
39. lamp	ramp	lump	lamp	romp	lamb
40. bright	fright	plight	right	blight	bright
41. fate	feat	fade	fail	fate	fact
42. law	law	low	raw	row	lawn
43. past	pest	past	best	post	pats
44. heal	hear	heel	heal	hale	deal
45. trail	tail	trial	rail	train	trail
46. lead	read	lad	lead	led	leap

47. strap	strip	traps	strap	start	stray
48. lose	loose	sole	lost	lose	loss
49. drops	props	drops	prods	drips	ropes
50. speed	speak	seed	sped	speed	deeps
51. cheese	crease	choose	chess	cheats	cheese
52. pots	tops	puts	lots	pots	spot
53. lunch	punch	lunch	hunch	launch	lurch
54. tile	tire	tail	tile	tide	till
55. scrap	strap	scrape	script	scrap	strip
56. bread	breed	dread	bred	beard	bread
57. sway	slay	ways	sway	swat	stay
58. fail	fail	sail	hall	fall	hail
59. shoes	choose	shoes	shows	hoes	shops
60. chore	shore	choir	chose	chore	core

TIME _____

SCORE _____

25

Name _____

Word Recognition—Continued

Directions: Do these problems the same way that you did the last ones.

TEST WORDS					
1. sing	sink	sins	sang	sign	sing
2. coves	caves	doves	cover	coves	cores
3. slip	sleep	slip	spill	slid	lips
4. robe	robs	rope	robe	rode	lobe
5. pain	gain	paint	pane	pain	pair
6. books	books	hooks	boots	looks	cooks
7. mild	mile	wild	mill	mind	mild
8. stars	stair	start	stars	store	stir
9. pole	pore	pole	bole	pale	polo
10. fought	sought	bought	fought	taught	naught
11. same	sane	shame	save	came	same
12. rate	mate	rats	rate	rote	late
13. lost	lots	last	lost	loss	lose
14. sets	sits	test	sees	sets	eats
15. four	your	four	tour	for	flour
16. boast	roast	boats	toast	boost	boast
17. tired	fired	tired	tried	tied	tiled
18. dark	dart	darn	dark	bark	hark
19. slaps	slaps	lapse	claps	slays	slabs
20. ripe	ride	rope	rips	ripe	ribs
21. pail	jail	bail	fail	paid	pail
22. leaf	lead	leave	leak	lean	leaf
23. dream	dread	cream	dream	drama	drain

24. bend	band	bend	bent	dent	bond
25. mine	nine	wine	mind	mine	fine
26. form	fork	form	farm	dorm	fore
27. must	most	mast	must	rust	muss
28. bear	beer	dear	bean	bear	bare
29. quite	quiet	quit	quite	quote	quilt
30. than	then	thin	them	that	than
31. claw	clam	claw	clew	clan	clay
32. door	deer	doer	door	odor	doom
33. sale	sail	salt	ales	sale	safe
34. read	real	lead	read	raid	rest
35. tune	tune	tone	tons	town	dune
36. slay	slab	slew	lays	stay	slay
37. grows	prows	grows	grown	glows	grass
38. much	such	must	hush	mush	much
39. wire	wise	were	mire	wire	hire
40. heard	heart	heard	hard	head	beard
41. tame	team	time	fame	tame	lame
42. mail	maid	nail	mail	mile	meal
43. gain	grain	pain	gale	gain	game
44. dime	time	dine	lime	dime	dune
45. fact	feat	fact	fast	face	tact
46. mine	mile	nine	mind	mire	mine
47. head	heed	heat	head	heal	hard
48. great	greet	grate	great	grade	green
49. halt	half	hall	hale	halt	held
50. load	load	lead	loaf	loan	road
51. dead	deed	dead	head	deal	bead
52. hate	hats	heat	hate	hale	have

28

53. male	mate	make	mats	male	meal
54. recent	reason	resent	recent	decent	season
55. swallow	shallow	swallow	wallow	hollow	swollen
56. report	resort	deport	report	porter	repast
57. matter	madder	matted	water	mutter	matter
58. robber	rubber	jobber	rudder	roller	robber
59. oven	even	over	omen	oven	ever
60. reading	reaping	leading	seeding	reading	ridding

TIME _____

SCORE _____

Name _____

Word-Pair Recognition

Directions: In each problem you are given a pair of phrases. Sometimes both phrases are exactly the same; sometimes they are different. If the two phrases are the *same,* underline the letter S. If the two phrases are *different,* underline the letter D.

Examples:

| doesn't know | doesn't show | S | D | [they are *different*] |
| have time | have time | S | D | [they are the *same*] |

Work as rapidly and as accurately as you can.

1. poor day   poor pay   S D
2. farm house   farm house   S D
3. new chair   new chair   S D
4. next door   next store   S D
5. choose one   choose one   S D
6. live alone   leave alone S D
7. not yet   not wet   S D
8. quick trip   quick trip   S D
9. bus stop   bus top   S D
10. wait longer wait longer S D
11. try hard   try hard   S D
12. pay day   play day   S D
13. write back   right back   S D
14. empty pen   empty pan   S D
15. fresh paint fresh paint S D
16. digs down   digs down   S D
17. hold tight   hold right   S D
18. wants more   wants more   S D

31

19. fast train	last train	S	D
20. quiet night	quite right	S	D
21. strong rope	strong rope	S	D
22. fresh fruit	fresh fruit	S	D
23. thick fog	thick log	S	D
24. walk fast	walk past	S	D
25. tight shoes	tight shoes	S	D
26. take mine	take time	S	D
27. new book	new look	S	D
28. walk out	watch out	S	D
29. small house	small house	S	D
30. make up	wake up	S	D
31. really nice	really nice	S	D
32. hardly ever	hardly even	S	D
33. so soon	go soon	S	D
34. call later	call later	S	D
35. short visit	short visit	S	D
36. look over	took over	S	D
37. wrong one	wrong one	S	D
38. full up	pull up	S	D
39. turn down	burn down	S	D
40. hot sun	hot sun	S	D
41. gets mail	get small	S	D
42. big town	big town	S	D
43. talk softly	walk softly	S	D
44. soft rain	soft rain	S	D
45. best choice	best choice	S	D
46. fall down	call down	S	D
47. sweet taste	sweet taste	S	D
48. good place	good plays	S	D

49. wet paint	wet paint	S	D
50. fire laws	fire loss	S	D
51. never ready	never ready	S	D
52. more shirts	wore shirts	S	D
53. loud noise	loud noise	S	D
54. pretty soon	pretty moon	S	D
55. deaf man	dead man	S	D
56. city streets	city streets	S	D
57. red rose	rose red	S	D
58. too early	too early	S	D
59. better day	wetter day	S	D
60. hear them	fear them	S	D

TIME _____

SCORE _____

PART THREE

Increasing Your Word-Comprehension Speed

In the last section you were given a series of exercises to increase your speed at responding to the appearance of English words and phrases. In this section the exercises are designed to give you practice in responding more quickly to the *meaning* of English words.

The vocabulary in these exercises will be extremely easy. You should therefore be able to work very quickly, without having to stop to think about the words in the problems, and certainly without having to translate them into your own language. You should try to develop the ability to respond automatically to the meaning of the words you encounter.

Name _____

Word Comprehension

Directions: Each problem consists of a "test word" followed by four possible meanings. Underline the word that means most nearly the same as the "test word."

Example:

      shut   watch   <u>close</u>   sleep   need

When you *shut* a door or a book, you *close* it. Therefore the verb *close* means about the same as the "test word," *shut.*

Work as rapidly and as accurately as you can.

1. speak	point	talk	hope	see
2. chair	paper	truth	hill	seat
3. begin	feel	leave	start	promise
4. near	pretty	small	real	close
5. receive	cry	get	wonder	mean
6. remain	stay	laugh	watch	trade
7. permit	smile	open	allow	move
8. fight	labor	ship	plant	battle
9. desire	open	want	marry	paint
10. little	small	brave	same	late
11. answer	reply	return	touch	save
12. simple	ready	short	easy	daily
13. large	yellow	round	big	middle
14. amusing	funny	straight	proper	real
15. labor	trip	work	strength	letter
16. strike	wait	trust	fear	hit
17. attempt	destroy	mention	try	die
18. people	gardens	methods	papers	folks
19. perhaps	always	maybe	truly	therefore
20. sick	full	true	different	ill
21. ship	mile	price	boat	world

22. obtain	get	turn	hang	enter
23. quick	modern	safe	fast	fresh
24. finish	guess	complete	grow	divide
25. lift	raise	practice	smile	meet
26. beneath	within	under	around	beside
27. several	nice	narrow	proud	some
28. center	middle	peace	school	path
29. request	wave	ask	ride	care
30. sufficient	possible	tall	broken	enough
31. certainly	usually	very	surely	suddenly
32. discover	refuse	sail	travel	find
33. lad	meat	roof	boy	harm
34. enjoy	like	offer	remove	surprise
35. occur	reach	happen	gather	thank
36. aid	help	pain	race	value
37. recall	trade	understand	throw	remember
38. road	shop	trouble	street	view
39. hurry	seek	taste	rush	wash
40. single	thin	one	wide	rich
41. noise	sound	maid	company	poem
42. silent	valuable	warm	still	human
43. imagine	tie	suppose	wait	obey
44. village	weather	voice	group	town
45. entire	young	whole	open	proper
46. liberty	freedom	mistake	family	method
47. observe	promise	pull	watch	turn
48. command	catch	order	burn	treat
49. correct	same	long	right	quiet
50. purchase	step	buy	listen	dream

TIME _____

SCORE _____

Name _____

Sames and Opposites

Directions: In each problem there are two words whose meanings are either approximately the same or approximately the opposite. If the two words have about the *same* meaning, underline the letter S. If they have *opposite* meanings, underline the letter O.

Examples:

| stop | go | S | <u>O</u> | [they mean the *opposite*] |
| speak | talk | <u>S</u> | O | [they mean the *same*] |

Work as rapidly and as accurately as you can.

1. dirty	clean	S O		19. cease	stop	S O	
2. journey	trip	S O		20. difficult	easy	S O	
3. late	early	S O		21. enjoy	like	S O	
4. rough	smooth	S O		22. future	past	S O	
5. hurt	injure	S O		23. dangerous	safe	S O	
6. narrow	wide	S O		24. almost	nearly	S O	
7. gift	present	S O		25. glad	happy	S O	
8. find	lose	S O		26. few	many	S O	
9. never	always	S O		27. long	short	S O	
10. joy	happiness	S O		28. full	empty	S O	
11. certain	sure	S O		29. ready	prepared	S O	
12. distant	near	S O		30. same	different	S O	
13. dine	eat	S O		31. public	private	S O	
14. sell	buy	S O		32. calm	quiet	S O	
15. war	peace	S O		33. much	little	S O	
16. work	rest	S O		34. consent	agree	S O	
17. tale	story	S O		35. dry	wet	S O	
18. succeed	fail	S O		36. cheap	expensive	S O	

37. forget	remember	S O	49. true	false	S O
38. choose	select	S O	50. depart	leave	S O
39. friend	enemy	S O	51. drop	lift	S O
40. enter	leave	S O	52. night	day	S O
41. huge	large	S O	53. employ	hire	S O
42. top	bottom	S O	54. tall	short	S O
43. strong	weak	S O	55. ugly	beautiful	S O
44. sorrow	joy	S O	56. alive	dead	S O
45. completely	entirely	S O	57. funny	amusing	S O
46. rich	poor	S O	58. under	over	S O
47. terrible	awful	S O	59. locate	find	S O
48. low	high	S O	60. awake	asleep	S O

TIME _____

SCORE _____

PART FOUR

Increasing Your
Sentence-Comprehension Speed

The exercises in the previous section were designed to give you practice in the rapid comprehension of isolated words. In this section you will be given two very different kinds of exercises to increase your speed at comprehending full sentences.

In these exercises you should try to read the sentences rapidly for their *general meaning* only. Do not attempt to consider each word by itself, for this bad reading habit will quickly affect both your speed and your comprehension.

Name _____

Sentence Completion

Directions: Each problem consists of a sentence with a word missing. You are then given four words, only one of which will complete the sentence in a logical way. Decide which word should be used in the sentence and draw a line under it.

Example:

You can trust Henry to take good care of your money, for he is very _____.

(a) angry   (b) <u>honest</u>   (c) evil   (d) distant

All the words in this exercise are easy ones. The object is to see how fast you can read the sentences and still understand what you are reading. Therefore work as rapidly and as accurately as you can.

1. After writing the letter, Paul found that he couldn't mail it because he had no _____.

    (a) paper   (b) friends   (c) stamps   (d) paint

2. If the coffee isn't sweet enough, I'll bring you some _____.

    (a) salt   (b) cream   (c) butter   (d) sugar

3. There was so much noise that Betty couldn't hear the man's angry _____.

    (a) shout   (b) wave   (c) cheer   (d) glance

4. None of the stores had the kind of shoes I wanted, so I didn't _____ any.

    (a) sell   (b) return   (c) buy   (d) save

5. You can't lock the door if you don't have a _____.

    (a) map   (b) key   (c) check   (d) sheet

6. If you want me to cut this rope, you'll have to get me a _____.

    (a) nail   (b) pole   (c) knife   (d) brush

7. It is too dark to read in here without a _____.

    (a) light   (b) pen   (c) book   (d) desk

8. I thought we still had some milk, but the bottle is _____.

    (a) level   (b) bare   (c) cold   (d) empty

9. Mary wanted to go to New York by herself, but her father and mother would not give their _____.

    (a) control   (b) example   (c) consent   (d) limit

10. I was surprised to meet Martha's husband, for I hadn't known that she was _____.

    (a) busy   (b) married   (c) angry   (d) single

11. If these shoes are too big, ask the clerk to bring you a smaller _____.

    (a) copy   (b) pair   (c) set   (d) amount

12. When George won the race, he received a silver cup as his _____.

    (a) fare   (b) debt   (c) prize   (d) charge

13. Clara wanted to buy the coat, but it cost more than she could _____.

    (a) assume   (b) afford   (c) arouse   (d) adopt

14. My father's youngest brother is my favorite _____.

    (a) uncle   (b) parent   (c) aunt   (d) cousin

15. I had hoped that Henry would answer my question, but he remained _____.

    (a) ready   (b) certain   (c) willing   (d) silent

16. It was easy to find seats in the train because there were so few _____.

    (a) tracks   (b) stations   (c) passengers   (d) tickets

17. The show should have started an hour ago; I don't know what could have caused the _____.

    (a) alarm   (b) delay   (c) statement   (d) custom

18. I sometimes take John's coat instead of my own, because the two of them look so _____.

    (a) original   (b) similar   (c) comfortable (d) curious

19. Robert must have liked the pie, because he asked for another _____.

    (a) piece   (b) edge   (c) length   (d) load

20. Paul likes ships and the sea so much that he has decided to become a _____.

    (a) servant   (b) soldier   (c) secretary   (d) sailor

21. No one could look in our windows if you would close the _____.

    (a) locks   (b) handles   (c) boxes   (d) curtains

22. The box was too heavy for the old woman to _____.

    (a) watch   (b) lift   (c) reach   (d) touch

23. I know it must be nearly dinner time because I'm getting very _____.

    (a) patient   (b) secure   (c) hungry   (d) sorry

24. I should finish the book tonight, for I've read all but the last _____.

    (a) copy   (b) title   (c) measure   (d) chapter

25. George had difficulty swimming across the lake, but he finally succeeded on his fourth _____.

    (a) attempt   (b) process   (c) display   (d) instance

26. Arthur was so badly hurt in the accident that they had to rush him to a _____.

    (a) library   (b) hospital   (c) factory   (d) theater

27. Since they had very little money to buy food, the family often had to go without _____.

    (a) exercise   (b) notice   (c) relief   (d) supper

45

28. Mary hated the farm so much that when her father came to take her back to the city, she felt very _____.

    (a) happy   (b) welcome   (c) angry   (d) sorry

29. I know that George Washington died in 1799, but I don't remember the year of his _____.

    (a) death   (b) life   (c) birth   (d) age

30. Last week's meeting was so long that they have promised that this one will be very _____.

    (a) complete   (b) brief   (c) fair   (d) narrow

31. The bird couldn't fly because one of its wings was _____.

    (a) perfect   (b) steady   (c) active   (d) broken

32. I am sure Mr. Smith would help you if he weren't so _____.

    (a) patient   (b) steady   (c) willing   (d) busy

33. You can't always believe everything Charles says, for he doesn't always tell the _____.

    (a) reason   (b) truth   (c) story   (d) time

34. Let Peter carry those heavy baskets; he's very _____.

    (a) weak   (b) tired   (c) strong   (d) direct

35. Dr. Brown can see you in half an hour if you care to _____.

    (a) speak   (b) wait   (c) hear   (d) leave

36. All these pictures are so beautiful that I don't know which one to _____.

    (a) lose   (b) need   (c) choose   (d) like

37. I thought the children would be sleeping when we returned home, but they were still _____.

    (a) awake   (b) quiet   (c) friendly   (d) apart

38. Potatoes seem to be Carl's favorite _____.

    (a) fruit   (b) flower   (c) vegetable   (d) grain

39. It is rather cold again today, but tomorrow we expect the temperature to _____.

(a) settle   (b) grow   (c) rise   (d) hold

40. Unless you have a good map, our village is very difficult to _____.

(a) accept   (b) locate   (c) preserve   (d) equal

41. I know I have seen that man before, I can't _____ where.

(a) assume   (b) wonder   (c) recognize   (d) recall

42. It will be easier to get across the river when they build the new _____.

(a) church   (b) bridge   (c) coast   (d) beach

43. If you still don't know what to do, I suggest you ask Paul's _____.

(a) example   (b) knowledge   (c) benefit   (d) advice

44. I don't know what happened at the meeting because I wasn't able to _____.

(a) decline   (b) apply   (c) depart   (d) attend

45. I want to go to the library, but I'm afraid I'm not walking in the right _____.

(a) distance   (b) circumstance   (c) attitude   (d) direction

46. I want to learn more about the American political system, but I don't know where to get the _____.

(a) situation   (b) information   (c) conversation   (d) association

47. Mrs. Wilson found that she couldn't do all the work in the house by herself, so she hired a _____.

(a) guide   (b) clerk   (c) maid   (d) chief

48. In this hot weather the ice will soon _____.

(a) spoil   (b) melt   (c) bake   (d) fail

49. It must have rained last night, for the grass is still _____.

    (a) warm   (b) weak   (c) wet   (d) worn

50. We had hoped that Robert would agree to help us, but he has _____ to.

    (a) desired   (b) promised   (c) refused   (d) intended

TIME _____

SCORE _____

Reading Sentences for General Meaning

Directions: In this exercise you are given 30 statements of the kind that might appear in reviews of a new book.

Put a *check mark* before each statement that suggests that the reviewer *approves* of the book.

Put a *circle* before each statement that seems to show that the reviewer *does not approve* of the book.

Examples:

    √   I would not hesitate to recommend Professor Baker's latest book to anyone who has even the slightest interest in this subject.

    O   There is little in Professor Baker's latest book that is new, and there is much that recent scientific studies have shown to be untrue.

Work as rapidly and as accurately as you can.

_____ 1. It is difficult to see how anyone could find Professor Baker's latest book anything but completely satisfying.

_____ 2. On page after page of Professor Baker's book I found statements which my own experience in this field would certainly lead me to question.

_____ 3. Although I have the highest personal regard for Professor Baker, I must confess that I find few major points in this book upon which he and I agree.

_____ 4. I regret that the high price of Professor Baker's latest book will prevent a work of such great merit from being as widely read as it surely deserves to be.

_____ 5. In spite of Professor Baker's excellent reputation in his field, I find it impossible to support the position which he takes in this, his most recent book.

_____ 6. Professor Baker states in the introduction to his latest book that it was four years in preparation; one wonders, then, why he did not check his facts with greater care.

_____ 7. I had supposed that no one would ever produce a book on this subject with which I would find myself in complete agreement; but Professor Baker has now done the impossible!

_____ 8. Since Professor Baker gathered the material for his latest book, a wealth of new evidence has been found which clearly shows how unsound are the judgments that he makes.

_____ 9. After reading and rereading Professor Baker's book with the greatest care, I simply cannot understand why some reviewers have found fault with the position which this distinguished teacher has taken.

_____ 10. After reading Professor Baker's latest book, I can only conclude that he was compelled by circumstances beyond his control to produce the work in such great haste as to be unable to check his facts in the customary way.

_____ 11. Professor Baker always expresses himself in a delightfully amusing manner; yet even _his_ clever style cannot conceal his lack of real understanding of the difficult subject on which he writes.

_____ 12. I should be very much surprised, indeed, if Professor Baker's newest book did not soon become the standard work in this field, a position which it so richly deserves.

_____ 13. It will be a great pity if Professor Baker's new book is read only by the experts in his field, for a writer of such high standards surely deserves a much wider audience.

_____ 14. It is hard to see how any intelligent reader could fail to be completely satisfied with Professor Baker's reasoning or with the conclusions he reaches in his latest book.

_____ 15. One cannot quarrel with the nature of the evidence which Professor Baker offers in his latest book; but at the same time one cannot honestly accept the conclusions which he reaches on the basis of this evidence.

_____ 16. It is curious how a writer who was once so careful with his facts and sound in his judgments could, as in the case of Professor Baker and his latest book, suddenly abandon his usual high standards and produce a work of such slight merit.

_____ 17. Although Professor Baker's most recent book contains fewer than 200 pages, I find it impossible to imagine how a better introduction to the subject could ever be produced.

_____ 18. One cannot help expressing regret that more writers in this difficult field do not have Professor Baker's gift of clear expression combined with his soundness of judgment.

_____ 19. In such a difficult field it is not often that one encounters a general treatment that is both sound in its theory and entertaining in its style; but Professor Baker's most recent book is one to which the above description can quite justly be applied.

_____ 20. Of Professor Baker's latest book I can say only that his and my views remain worlds apart, and though I yield to no one in my admiration for his smooth-flowing literary style, my opinions of what he has to say are quite another matter.

_____ 21. Other reviewers, I find, have had some very unkind things to say about this, Professor Baker's most recent book; for my own part, I really cannot imagine how this little volume could be improved upon in any substantial way.

_____ 22. Professor Baker's publisher has stated that this new book will soon take the place of all the old standard works in this field; in view, however, of both the style and content of Professor Baker's book, I find this claim most difficult to accept.

_____ 23. In today's world it becomes increasingly essential for all men to acquire some knowledge and understanding of science; but to such understanding the latest book of Professor Baker will, alas, contribute very little.

_____ 24. No one in this field can read Professor Baker's latest book without feeling the deepest regret over the early death of a scientist whose ability as a writer is no less remarkable than his well-known skill in the university classroom.

_____ 25. There is certainly a great need in this field for a short, general survey which combines sound scientific theory with good literary style; but, though no one could find fault with Professor Baker's style, the theory which he advances in this, his most recent book, leaves a great deal to be desired.

_____ 26. It is the policy of this journal to allow its reviewers no more than four hundred words to discuss any new book; but for me to do justice to a work of such high quality as Professor Baker's latest volume would require a review fully ten times that length.

_____ 27. In my previous review of the books in this difficult field, I expressed the opinion that no satisfactory treatment of the subject had ever been published; and after reading Professor Baker's latest attempt in the same area, I am compelled to report that the situation remains unchanged.

_____ 28. I shall review two books published recently in this field, beginning with that by Professor Baker, which, though very much the smaller of the two, seems to me to present by far the better treatment, and, indeed, to provide the beginning student with an ideal introduction to this difficult subject.

_____ 29. When I first opened the package containing a copy of Professor Baker's latest book and read its title, I must admit I felt a sudden sinking of the heart; yet once I had gathered courage to begin my reading, I found the work so far beyond my wildest hopes that I actually missed supper rather than put the volume down unfinished.

_____ 30. In his latest book Professor Baker has endeavored to present the beginning student with a popular introduction to his subject, and, although I am certainly in full sympathy with his purpose, I must in all honesty report that here, as in so many popular treatments in the field of science, the efforts to give a simple yet true picture of a difficult subject have proved to be far beyond the capacity of the writer.

TIME _____

SCORE _____

PART FIVE

Reading Paragraphs for Central Idea

In the previous lessons you were given exercises to help you increase your speed in comprehending isolated words and sentences. In this and subsequent lessons we shall be concerned with the rapid comprehension of longer units of writing—the paragraph and the complete composition.

How we read these longer units will depend both on our *purpose* in reading and on the *level of difficulty* of the material. In some cases it is enough if we simply comprehend the writer's main ideas, without devoting much attention to the minor details. Much of the reading we do for general information or for pleasure is of this kind— the reading of magazine and newspaper articles, for example. It is also the technique we would probably use in "skimming" reference books in order to determine whether they are sufficiently important for our purposes to merit a more careful and thorough reading.

On the other hand, classroom textbooks and other complex materials must often be read both for central idea or ideas, and for the supporting details. In such cases it is frequently advisable to read the material twice—once to comprehend the writer's main thoughts and a second time to understand the detail, such as the steps the writer uses to reach his conclusion, the evidence he gives in support of his argument, or the illustrations he provides to help us understand a general principle.

Clearly, then, a first step in increasing our skill in reading longer passages is to practice reading rapidly for central idea. In this lesson we shall apply this technique to a series of short, unrelated paragraphs. The effective method of reading for central idea may be briefly summarized as follows:

1. Force yourself to read the paragraphs a little faster than you are used to doing. Normally when you read, you are concerned with comprehending both the central idea and the supporting detail. This time, however, your purpose is solely to find the writer's main thought. Therefore you should be able to read somewhat faster. On the other hand, do not attempt to skim so rapidly that you risk losing altogether the sense of what you are reading. Try for a reading speed that is only a little faster than usual.
2. Concentrate on finding, and following, the writer's central idea. Do not attempt to remember details such as exact dates, lists of names, large numbers, and the like.
3. If you find an occasional word which you do not understand, or lose the sense of a word or phrase here and there, do not stop to reread the material. Continue reading at the slightly faster than normal speed that you have established.

Now try to apply the above technique to the exercise that follows.

Reading for Central Idea

Directions: This exercise consists of ten paragraphs, each on a different subject. Read each paragraph quickly to determine the central idea. Then turn the page and check the one statement which best expresses the central idea. In deciding on your answer, *do not look back at the paragraph.* As soon as you have marked your answer, go on to the next paragraph. Work as rapidly and as accurately as you can.

Name _____

Paragraph one

Most civilizations and cultures—in their sacred writings, in their oral traditions, in their folk stories—have some reference to the origin of language. Only rarely (at least in the records that have come down to us) did the ancients try to learn something about speech phenomena by observation or experimentation. The Greek historian Herodotus (fifth century B.C.) records one such incident: an Egyptian king named Psammetichos wished to determine which of the world's languages was oldest. To gain this information, he decided to isolate two newborn infants until such time as they should begin to speak; the assumption being that, lacking any pattern to imitate, they would therefore naturally employ the most primitive of the languages. In the course of time the children were heard to utter something that was recorded as *bekos*—which turned out to be similar to the Phrygian word for "bread." Therefore, Phrygian (a language once spoken in Asia Minor) was held to be the first language of mankind, at least by King Psammetichos and, we may presume, by his court.

(Now turn the page and mark the sentence that most nearly expresses the central idea of the paragraph.)

Adapted from *Perspectives in Linguistics* by John T. Waterman. Copyright 1963 by The University of Chicago Press. All rights reserved. Reprinted by permission of The University of Chicago.

The central idea of paragraph one is:

_____ (a) Psammetichos concluded that the first word that children speak is the word for "bread."

_____ (b) Psammetichos concluded that Phrygian was the oldest language in the world.

_____ (c) Psammetichos concluded that the oldest word in any language is the word for "bread."

_____ (d) Psammetichos concluded that Phrygian was the easiest language in the world to learn.

Paragraph two

Some of the notebooks that George Washington kept as a young man are still in existence, and they show that he learned a little Latin, that he acquired some of the basic elements of good conduct, and that he read a little English literature. At school he seems to have cared only for mathematics. His was a brief and most incomplete education for a gentleman, and it was all the formal education he was to have, since, unlike some of the other young Virginia gentlemen of his time, he did not go on to the College of William and Mary in the Virginia capital of Williamsburg. In terms of intellectual preparation and power, then, Washington is in sharp contrast with some other early American presidents, such as John Adams, Thomas Jefferson, and James Madison. In later years, Washington probably regretted his lack of intellectual training. He never felt comfortable in formal debate, or in discussions that were not concerned with everyday, practical matters. And inasmuch as he never learned to speak French, he refused to visit France because he felt he would be embarrassed at not being able to speak directly to the statesmen of that country. Thus, unlike Jefferson and Adams, he never reached Europe.

The central idea of paragraph two is:

_____ (a) Washington's education showed unusual variety, including as it did, study in fields as varied as mathematics and literature.

_____ (b) Washington's education was probably equal to that obtained by other Virginia gentlemen of his age.

_____ (c) Washington's education may seem limited by modern standards, but it appears to have been entirely adequate for the duties of his later years.

_____ (d) Washington's education was extremely limited and probably put him at a disadvantage in later life.

Name _____

Most American folk songs are importations. Brought over by the settlers, influenced by new living conditions, changed to reflect another scene and setting, they still show their origins. Under different titles, and celebrating another set of characters, the story songs of Vermont and the mountain tunes of the Appalachians are largely adaptations of such English and Scottish ballads as "Barbara Allen," "The Hangman's Song," "The Two Sisters," and "Lord Randal." But a few—and perhaps the best—of the American ballads are genuinely native, as original in subject as they are lively in expression. Beginning as reports of local events or current beliefs or merely as play songs, they have become part of the national life. The five most vivid are also the most popular: "Dixie," "My Old Kentucky Home," "Frankie and Johnny,' "Casey Jones," and "John Henry." Unlike most folk songs, the authors of at least two of them are known.

Adapted from *A Treasury of Great Poems, English and American* edited by Louis Untermeyer, 1942. Reprinted by permission of Simon and Schuster, Inc.

61

The central idea of paragraph three is:

_____ (a) Most American folk songs are simply variations of older ballads imported from abroad, though a few of the best and most popular are American originals.

_____ (b) Such vivid and popular folk songs as "Frankie and Johnny" and "John Henry" are really only adaptations of much older English and Scottish ballads.

_____ (c) Although the authors of most American folk songs are unknown, a few can definitely be identified.

_____ (d) American folk songs are unlike those of other countries because of differences in living conditions, settings, and local events.

Paragraph four

The question has sometimes been raised whether Shakespeare knew Greek. The masters of the Stratford school which Shakespeare attended were no doubt well qualified to teach Greek. But the question, after all, is idle since there is no reason whatever to believe that Shakespeare read Greek or had any acquaintance with Greek literature—except Plutarch—either in the original or in translation. With Latin, however, the case is different. When we read Jonson's statement that Shakespeare had "small Latin," we must remember that what seemed like little Latin to such a scholar as Johnson would be a very respectable quantity today. A boy would have been dull indeed who could spend six or seven years devoted almost entirely to the study of Latin for about ten hours a day and yet emerge from the process without a very fair command of the language.

Adapted from *Shakespeare: Twenty-Three Plays and the Sonnets* edited by Thomas Marc Parrott, 1953. Reprinted by permission of Charles Scribner's Sons.

The central idea of paragraph four is:

_____ (a) The fact that Shakespeare learned neither Greek nor Latin suggests that he was a dull student.

_____ (b) Because Shakespeare was a dull boy, he had to spend six or seven years studying almost nothing but Latin.

_____ (c) Shakespeare probably had no greater knowledge of Latin than he had of Greek.

_____ (d) We may conclude that Shakespeare could not read Greek but probably had a very satisfactory knowledge of Latin.

Paragraph five

The large part which war played in English affairs in the Middle Ages, the fact that the control of the army and navy was in the hands of those who spoke French, and the circumstances that much of English fighting was done in France all resulted in the introduction into English of a number of French military terms. The art of war has undergone such changes since the battles of Hastings, Lewes, and Agincourt that many words once common are now only in historical use. Their places have been taken by later borrowings, often likewise from French, many of them being words acquired by the French in the course of their wars in Italy during the sixteenth century. Nevertheless we still use French words of the Middle Ages when we speak of the *army* and the *navy*, of *peace, enemy, battle, soldier, guard,* and *spy,* and we have kept the names of officers such as *captain, lieutenant,* and *sergeant.* Some of the French terms were introduced into English because they were needed to identify a new object or express a new idea. In other cases a French and a native English word for the same thing existed side by side. Sometimes one or the other has since been lost from the language; but sometimes (as in the case of the pair *battle* and *fight*) both the borrowed and the native word have been retained in common use.

Adapted from *A History of the English Language,* 2nd Ed., by Albert C. Baugh. Copyright © 1957 by Appleton-Century-Crofts, Inc. Reprinted by permission of Appleton-Century-Crofts, Inc. and the author.

The central idea of paragraph five is:

_____ (a) Most of today's common English military terms date from the sixteenth century or later.

_____ (b) A study of the English vocabulary shows the important part which warfare has played in England's history.

_____ (c) Many French words borrowed into English during the Middle Ages have since disappeared from the language.

_____ (d) Many military terms used in English were originally borrowed from French, some as early as the Middle Ages.

Paragraph six

Architecture, then, is an art, and any art must give us pleasure, or else it is bad art, or we are abnormally blind. We are in general too hardened and insensitive to architecture as an art and to the joy it may bring to us. It is the constant nearness of architecture during our entire conscious existence that has blinded us in this way. We forget that it is an art of here and now, because it is with us every day, and because we must have houses to live in we are apt to think of them solely as abiding places. Therefore we think of architecture as some vague, learned thing dealing with French cathedrals or Italian palaces or Greek temples, not with New York or Chicago streets or Los Angeles suburbs, and this false doctrine has strengthened in us until our eyes are dulled and our minds are deadened to all the beauty that is being created around us today, and we lose all the fine deep pleasure that we might otherwise experience from our ordinary surroundings.

Adapted from *Architecture: An Art for All Men* by Talbot Hamlin, 1947. Reprinted by permission of Columbia University Press.

The central idea of paragraph six is:

_____ (a) Although some modern architecture is truly art, much of the new building is more useful than it is beautiful.

_____ (b) It is naturally difficult for people used to the dull architecture of a New York or Chicago to understand fully the ancient monuments of Europe.

_____ (c) In our daily lives we are so completely surrounded by architecture that we have ceased to see and enjoy it as art.

_____ (d) Architecture must surely be considered an art, for throughout our daily lives we are constantly deriving pleasure from it.

Paragraph seven

A decade prior to their defeat of the Spanish Armada, the English made their first attempts to colonize America. Securing in 1578 royal permission for exploration and settlement, Sir Humphrey Gilbert twice set out for America. His first expedition was scattered by a storm, and on his second, in 1583, his frail vessel disappeared. Gilbert's half-brother, Sir Walter Raleigh, then took up the task and spent the remainder of his life and his large fortune in an effort to plant a settlement. His first expedition, in 1584, brought back glowing reports of the coast of Virginia; a second sent over the following year to plant a colony returned in discouragement; and a third, left isolated on the island of Roanoke, disappeared from history, leaving as the only evidence the word "Croatoan" carved on a tree. With his fortune exhausted, Raleigh retired from active colonization, but he remained until his death a strong supporter of English expansion.

The central idea of paragraph seven is:

_____ (a) If it had not been for the knowledge he gained from Gilbert's expeditions, Raleigh would probably have been far less successful in his explorations of the American coast.

_____ (b) Although Raleigh was more successful than Gilbert in exploring the American coast, his efforts at colonization ended in failure, too.

_____ (c) Gilbert and Raleigh are remembered as the first Englishmen to conduct successful explorations of the American coast.

_____ (d) Both Gilbert and Raleigh, the first two Englishmen to attempt the settlement of America, lost their lives in the course of their explorations.

Name _____

It has been estimated that only about twenty thousand words are in full use in English today, and if this estimate is correct, it brings us up to Shakespeare's total. Of these, one-fifth, or about four thousand, are said to be of Anglo-Saxon origin, and three-fifths, or about twelve thousand, are of Latin, Greek and French origin. This, of course, does not mean that our everyday conversation consists chiefly of foreign words. According to one estimate, one-fourth of all our spoken language consists of repetitions of the words *and, be, have, it, of, the, to, will, you, I, a, on, that,* and *is.* Another analysis of five million words written by adults reveals that our ten most frequently used words are *I, the, and, to, of, in, we, for, you* and *a.* Both lists consist, without exception, of native words. If we go into literary usage, we find that words of the Bible are ninety-four per cent native, Shakespeare's ninety per cent, Tennyson's eighty-eight per cent, Milton's eighty-one per cent, and Samuel Johnson's seventy-two per cent. Only in present-day technical writings do we find the foreign element climbing to forty per cent.

Adapted from *The Story of English* by Mario Pei. Copyright 1952 by Mario Pei. Reprinted by permission of J. B. Lippincott Company.

The central idea of paragraph eight is:

_____ (a) The words most frequently used in English conversation and literature are native.

_____ (b) English literature makes greater use of foreign words than does ordinary conversation.

_____ (c) Scientific writing in English contains a very high percentage of foreign words.

_____ (d) Some of the commonest words in English have been borrowed from Latin, Greek, and French.

Paragraph nine

In the 1840's and 1850's, America developed the famous clipper ships, the fastest sailing vessels the world had ever known. These graceful, three-masted ships were built mostly in New England shipyards, and they carried goods and people to every part of the world. During the era of the clipper ships the United States rapidly developed its merchant marine until it was the second largest in the world. With the commencement of the American Civil War, however, ocean commerce was reduced and fewer ships were built. The Southern navy destroyed many Northern merchant vessels, and the historic battle between the Monitor and the Merrimac proved that iron ships were going to take the place of wooden vessels. The United States never did build iron ships on as large a scale as it had built the clipper ships. After the war there was a tendency on the part of American businessmen and bankers to invest their money in railroads and other industries rather than in ocean shipping.

Adapted from *The Building of Our Nation* by E. C. Barker, *et al.*, 1951. Reprinted by permission of Harper & Row, Publishers.

The central idea of paragraph nine is:

_____ (a) It was some time after the Civil War that American shipping regained the position it had held in the days of the clipper ships.

_____ (b) After the Civil War the American clipper ships were gradually replaced by even larger and faster iron vessels.

_____ (c) Because of their great speed, the clipper ships proved as useful during the American Civil War as they had in peacetime.

_____ (d) The disappearance of the clipper ships and a general decline in American ocean shipping began during the Civil War.

Paragraph ten

Until the War of 1812, the United States had always bought its manufactured goods, especially its fine cloth, from England. During the war, however, the United States could neither sell its raw materials nor buy manufactured goods in European markets. There was nothing to do but manufacture its own goods. By the end of the War of 1812 there were nearly 150,000 men and women working in cotton and woolen mills in the United States. We have no figures on the number of workers employed in the various stages of iron production, but we know that the iron industry had greatly increased. Besides the cloth and iron works, there was a great leather industry, including shoe factories, saddle shops, and harness-making shops, while American hatters were able to supply the market for wool hats and fur caps.

Adapted from *The Building of Our Nation* by E. C. Barker, *et al.*, 1951. Reprinted by permission of Harper & Row, Publishers.

The central idea of paragraph ten is:

_____ (a) As a result of the War of 1812, Americans began to produce better cloth than they had previously obtained from abroad.

_____ (b) The War of 1812 caused large numbers of Americans to move from the farms into the factories.

_____ (c) After the War of 1812 the United States was far less dependent on Europe for its manufactured goods.

_____ (d) The War of 1812 caused a temporary change in the pattern of trade between the United States and Europe.

TIME _____

SCORE _____

PART SIX

Reading Paragraphs for Full Understanding

In the previous section you were given practice in reading paragraphs for their central idea. In this section you will be given another series of short passages, but this time you will be asked to read for total comprehension—that is, for an understanding both of the central idea and of the supporting details. Although this kind of *intensive reading* will probably require a slightly slower speed than did your reading for central idea only, you should still try to cover the material as rapidly as you can without losing the sense of what you are reading. If you read at a fairly rapid pace, you will find it easier to concentrate on *ideas* and the relations between ideas. The slow reader usually concerns himself too much with individual words and thus may actually comprehend less than the quick reader.

If, as you read, you come to a term that is not familiar to you, do not stop to puzzle over it; continue reading, and quite likely the general meaning of the sentence will become clear to you.

And finally, try to avoid going back and rereading words and phrases. Readers who make a habit of rereading parts of sentences generally harm, rather than help, their comprehension. Force yourself to concentrate on understanding everything the first time, and you will soon improve both your reading speed and your comprehension.

Exercise 11

Paragraph Comprehension

Directions: This is an exercise to test your ability to understand the meaning of paragraphs and short passages of English. Each problem consists of a passage followed on the next page by two comprehension questions. First read the paragraph, then turn the page and answer the questions by putting a check mark before the correct answer. Once you have started to answer a set of questions, *do not look back at the passage.* Answer the questions on the basis of what you remember about the passage. Work as rapidly and as accurately as you can.

ly increased, both in the United States
invention of a machine to remove the
which grew abundantly in the southern
States. This machine was the work of Eli
an from New England who had gone south
hile visiting a plantation, he heard a good
the cost of separating cotton fiber from the
seed. He was told that a man, working all day, could separate
only a pound of cotton from the seed. Both Georgia and South
Carolina had offered a prize for a machine that could do the
work, but no one had claimed it. Whitney became so much
interested in the problem that he quit teaching and put all his
time into the effort of inventing a cotton gin. In 1793 he completed a machine with which a man could clean fifty pounds
of cotton a day. He wrote his father proudly: "It makes the
labor fifty times less without throwing any class of people out
of business." He continued to work on his machine, improving it so that it would clean more and more cotton. But his
hopes of making a great fortune with the cotton gin were never
realized, because many people, after learning how, simply built
gins and paid Whitney nothing for his invention.

Adapted from *The Building of Our Nation* by E. C. Barker, *et al.*, 1951. Reprinted by
permission of Harper & Row, Publishers.

Questions on passage one:

1. How much cotton per day could be cleaned by one of Whitney's first machines?
   _____ (a) 5 pounds   _____ (c) 50 pounds
   _____ (b) 15 pounds   _____ (d) 150 pounds

2. Why did Whitney fail to make a fortune with his machine?
   _____ (a) Because the people of the South were slow to adopt it.
   _____ (b) Because other people copied it without paying him anything.
   _____ (c) Because he spent all his money trying to improve his original machine.
   _____ (d) Because other people invented machines that were much better.

Passage two

The Mother Goose stories, so well known to children all over the world, are commonly said to have been written by a little old woman for her grandchildren. According to some people, she lived in Boston, and her real name was Elizabeth Vergoose. Her son-in-law, a printer named Thomas Fleet, was supposed to have published the famous nursery stories and rhymes in 1719. However, no copy of this book has ever been found, and most scholars doubt the truth of this story—and doubt, moreover, that Mother Goose was ever a real person. They point out that the name is a direct translation of the French "Mère l'Oye." In 1697 the Frenchman Charles Perrault published the first book in which this name was used. The collection contains eight tales, including "Sleeping Beauty," "Cinderella," and "Puss in Boots." But Perrault did not originate these stories; they were already quite popular in his day, and he only collected them.

Questions on passage two:

3. What is supposed to have happened in 1719?
   - _____ (a) Elizabeth Vergoose composed the first Mother Goose stories.
   - _____ (b) Thomas Fleet published the Mother Goose stories.
   - _____ (c) The Mother Goose stories were translated into French.
   - _____ (d) Charles Perrault published the first Mother Goose stories.

4. On the basis of this passage, what may we conclude about the real origin of the stories "Sleeping Beauty" and "Cinderella"?
   - _____ (a) They were invented by Elizabeth Vergoose.
   - _____ (b) They were invented by Thomas Fleet.
   - _____ (c) They were invented by Charles Perrault.
   - _____ (d) Their authors are unknown.

Passage three

Early scholars in Europe and America assumed that the American Indian came from the Old World. After Russian explorers in the north Pacific Ocean made it clear that Alaska almost touched the mainland of Asia, wise men said the Indian came from that continent. You will find such statements in the oldest books upon the subject. In 1739 a great portrait painter named Smibert came to Boston to paint the colonial governors. He had painted at the Russian Court and so was familiar with the Siberians who appeared there from time to time. When Smibert saw the Indians he declared them to be Mongolians. From that day to this, everything points to a Mongoloid ancestry for the American Indian. Even the oldest human bones found in America have been pronounced Mongoloid. So one question is answered: the first man to discover America came from Siberia. This may not be the final answer, but since nothing to oppose it has been discovered since the time of Columbus, we must accept it as the best answer.

Adapted from *Indians of the United States* by Clark Wissler. Copyright 1940 by Doubleday & Company, Inc. Reprinted by permission of Doubleday & Company, Inc.

Questions on passage three:

5. Why had Smibert gone to Boston in 1739?
   _____ (a) To study the Indians who lived there.
   _____ (b) To sell the pictures he had painted in Russia.
   _____ (c) To deliver lectures on his theories about the Indians.
   _____ (d) To paint pictures of some high officials.

6. According to the writer, what *first* led wise men to conclude that the American Indian came from Asia?
   _____ (a) The evidence of the oldest bones to be found in America.
   _____ (b) Smibert's comparison of the Indians with Siberians.
   _____ (c) The discoveries of Russian explorers in the Pacific.
   _____ (d) Columbus's accounts of his travels to America.

Passage four

Basketball is one sport—perhaps the only sport—whose exact origin can safely be stated. During the winter of 1891-1892, Dr. James Naismith, a college instructor in Springfield, Massachusetts, invented the game of basketball in order to provide exercise for the students between the closing of the football season and the opening of the baseball season. He attached fruit baskets overhead on the walls at opposite ends of the gymnasium, and, using a soccer ball, organized nine-man teams to play his new game in which the purpose was to toss the ball into one basket and attempt to keep the opposing team from tossing the ball into the other basket. Although there have since been many changes in the rules (such as the reduction of the number of players on a team from nine to five), the game is basically the same today. United States soldiers introduced it to the Philippines in 1900 and to Europe during World War I, and, being adopted by foreign nations, it soon became a worldwide sport. It is interesting that although basketball was created as an indoor game, in countries other than the United States it is now played almost entirely outdoors.

Questions on passage four:

7. What does the writer say is particularly unusual about basketball as compared with other sports?
   _____ (a) It began as an indoor game but later became
   equally common as an outdoor game.
   _____ (b) We know exactly when, where, and by whom it
   was invented.
   _____ (c) It was invented for college students but became
   popular only after it was adopted by soldiers.
   _____ (d) We know exactly when it was first played outside
   of the country of its origin.

8. What connection does the writer mention between the game of
   basketball and the game of soccer?
   _____ (a) Basketball was first played with a soccer ball.
   _____ (b) Basketball has replaced soccer as the most popular
   sport in some countries.
   _____ (c) Basketball was invented by a well-known soccer
   player.
   _____ (d) Basketball was designed to provide exercise for
   students before the beginning of the soccer season.

Passage five

Many large birds possessing great powers of flight are, when not occupied with the business of raising their young, constantly wandering from place to place in search of food. They fly at a great height, and cover tremendous distances. In such regions as this, uncountable numbers of birds are, without doubt, constantly passing over us unseen. It was once the subject of very great wonder to me that flocks of black-necked swans should almost always appear flying by immediately after a shower of rain, even when none had been visible for a long time before, and when they must have come from a very great distance. When the reason at length occurred to me, I felt very much disgusted with myself for being puzzled over so very simple a matter. After rain a flying swan may be visible to the eye at a vastly greater distance than during fair weather, the sun shining on its intense white feathers against the dark background of a rain-cloud making it exceedingly conspicuous. The fact that swans are almost always seen after rain shows only that they are almost always passing.

Adapted from *The Naturalist in La Plata* by W. H. Hudson.

Questions on passage five:

9. According to the writer, why did he usually see flocks of black-necked swans after showers of rain?

_____ (a) Because it was easier for them to find food just after a rain.

_____ (b) Because, being water birds, they preferred to fly in the rain.

_____ (c) Because they were much easier to see against the dark sky of a rainy day.

_____ (d) Because after a rain they would fly to dry out their feathers.

10. What were the writer's first feelings when he discovered why he almost always saw the swans after a rain?

_____ (a) He was very proud to have added to the scientific knowledge of birds.

_____ (b) He wondered why he hadn't solved so easy a problem much sooner.

_____ (c) He realized how very little he really knew about the habits of birds.

_____ (d) He was amused to find how simple the explanation really was.

Passage six

When Turner's picture of the city of Cologne was exhibited in the year 1826, it hung between two of Sir Thomas Lawrence's portraits, one of Lady Wallscourt and the other of Lady Robert Manners. The sky of Turner's picture was extremely bright, and it had a most injurious effect on the color of the two portraits. Lawrence naturally was greatly disturbed, and complained openly of the position of his pictures. On the morning of the opening of the exhibition, at a private showing of the pictures, a friend of Turner's who had seen the Cologne, in all its splendor, led a group of expectant critics up to the picture. He started back from it in shocked amazement. The golden sky had changed to a dull brown. He ran up to Turner crying, "Turner, what have you been doing to your picture?" "Oh," muttered Turner, in a low voice, "poor Lawrence was so unhappy. It's only lamp-black.[1] It will all wash off after the exhibition."

---

[1] LAMP-BLACK: a black powder used to make paints.

Adapted from *Lectures on Architecture and Painting* by John Ruskin.

Questions on passage six:

11. According to the passage, why was Lawrence so disturbed to find Turner's picture hanging between his own?
    _____ (a) It was too bright.
    _____ (b) It was not a portrait.
    _____ (c) It was too large.
    _____ (d) It was obviously so much better than his own.

12. What quality of Turner's does this story best illustrate?
    _____ (a) His pride.
    _____ (b) His desire for praise.
    _____ (c) His artistic skill.
    _____ (d) His kindness.

Passage seven

    For my part, I could easily do without the post office. I think there are very few important communications made through it. To speak critically, I never received more than one or two letters in my life that were worth the postage. And I am sure that I never read any memorable news in a newspaper. If we read of one man robbed, or murdered, or killed by accident, or one house burned, or one vessel wrecked, or one cow run over on the Western Railroad, or one mad dog killed,—we never need read of another. One is enough. If you are acquainted with the principle, what do you care for ten thousand instances and applications? To a philosopher, all *news*, as it is called, is gossip,[1] and those who edit and those who read it are old women over their tea. There was such a rush, I have heard, the other day at one of the newspaper offices to learn the latest foreign news, that several large plate glass windows were broken by the pressure—yet it was news which I seriously think a clever man might write a year or twelve years beforehand with sufficient accuracy.

[1] GOSSIP: worthless talk which has little or no truth.

Adapted from *Walden* by Henry David Thoreau.

Questions on passage seven:

13. Why does the writer say he doesn't read newspapers?
    - _____ (a) Because they contain too much sadness and violence.
    - _____ (b) Because there is no way to prove that they tell the truth.
    - _____ (c) Because he is kept too busy reading and writing letters.
    - _____ (d) Because they never contain anything new or important.

14. What was the writer's main purpose in telling how "several large plate glass windows were broken"?
    - _____ (a) To illustrate men's foolish eagerness to learn what they regard as "news."
    - _____ (b) To illustrate how angry men may become upon learning bad news.
    - _____ (c) To illustrate the kind of minor event that is commonly reported in newspapers.
    - _____ (d) To illustrate the kind of violence that occurs every day.

Passage eight

There is one element in El Greco's paintings that has been largely ignored by modern critics, yet perhaps more than any other single quality it subconsciously has the greatest effect in pleasing the modern eye. It is his constant use of what can only be called "sophisticated" colors. The Renaissance masters, especially Raphael, used richly harmonious colors and color combinations that are immediately and universally appealing. But for that very reason they soon begin to lose their interest. Too steady a diet of deep or clear reds, sky blues, sunny yellows, instantly satisfying greens, and rich glowing purples tend to bore the modern viewer, and the eyes turn with fresh interest to a more subtle and unusual color range. El Greco seldom employs a simple green or yellow; in a skillful interplay of light and shadow each is always lightly blended with the other. His reds and pinks are softened by a mixture of blue or made harsh with orange. The resulting tones sometimes are placed side by side in oddly satisfying combinations. Yet he is never guilty of handling colors for mere shock value or in a strained way to be "different." There is always a definite artistic purpose behind his unusual methods—both purpose and methods abundantly justified in works of genius.

Adapted from *Enjoying Modern Art* by Sarah Newmeyer, 1957. Reprinted by permission of The New American Library of World Literature, Inc.

Questions on passage eight:

15. How does the writer describe El Greco's colors?
    _____ (a) Obviously chosen for their "shock value."
    _____ (b) Richly harmonious.
    _____ (c) Subtle and unusual.
    _____ (d) Immediately and universally appealing.

16. What point does the writer make about Raphael's colors?
    _____ (a) They help to explain the Renaissance masters' continuing popularity.
    _____ (b) After a while they begin to lose their interest.
    _____ (c) They are much more appreciated today than they were during Raphael's own age.
    _____ (d) They are difficult for the modern viewer to accept.

Passage nine

George Washington is the last person you would ever suspect of having been a young man, with all the bright hopes and black despairs which all young men feel. In American folk tales he is known only as a child or a general or an old, old man. By some trick of fate, Gilbert Stuart's "Athenaeum" portrait of an ideal and impressive, but solemn and weary, Washington at the age of sixty-four has become the most popular. It has been reproduced as the "official" portrait and placed in every school in the country; so we may expect that generations of American schoolchildren will be brought up with the idea that Washington was a solemn old bore. If only Charles Willson Peale's portrait of him as a handsome and gallant soldier could have been used instead! Or one of the charming little pictures that show him as a young man rejoicing in his strength! His older writers, too, have sought to create the legend; and the recent efforts to "popularize" Washington have unfortunately tried to present him as something that he was not: a churchman, politician, engineer, businessman.

Adapted from *The Young Washington* by Samuel Eliot Morison, 1932. Reprinted by permission of Harvard University Press.

Questions on passage nine:

17. What is the central idea of this paragraph?

———— (a) That Washington's many accomplishments have made him one of America's greatest popular heroes.

———— (b) That the picture which most Americans have of Washington is really false and incomplete.

———— (c) That recent historians have done much to correct the wrong ideas we once had of Washington.

———— (d) That in spite of what older writers and painters have done, Washington continues to command our respect.

18. Why does the writer object to the use of the present "official" portrait of Washington?

———— (a) Because it has never had truly popular appeal.

———— (b) Because the writer feels that official pictures tend, in time, to make people bored with the subject.

———— (c) Because the painter, Gilbert Stuart, lacked the artistic ability of some other painters of Washington.

———— (d) Because it shows Washington as old and tired.

Passage ten

Mrs. Bennet rang the bell, and Miss Elizabeth was summoned to the library.

"Come here, child," cried her father as she appeared. "I understand that Mr. Collins has made you an offer of marriage. Is it true?" Elizabeth replied that it was. "Very well—and this offer of marriage you have refused?"

"I have, sir."

"Very well. We now come to the point. Your mother insists upon your accepting it. Is it not so, Mrs. Bennet?"

"Yes, or I will never see her again."

"An unhappy choice is before you, Elizabeth. From this day you must be a stranger to one of your parents. Your mother will never see you again if you do *not* marry Mr. Collins, and I will never see you again if you *do.*"

Adapted from *Pride and Prejudice* by Jane Austen.

Questions on passage ten:

19. What had apparently been happening *immediately before* this
passage?
    - _____ (a) Mr. Bennet had been talking with Mrs. Bennet.
    - _____ (b) Mrs. Bennet had been talking with Elizabeth.
    - _____ (c) Elizabeth had been talking with Mr. Collins.
    - _____ (d) Mr. Bennet had been talking with Elizabeth.

20. What do we learn about Mr. Bennet from this conversation?
    - _____ (a) That he is afraid Elizabeth will leave home if she
      marries.
    - _____ (b) That he agrees with his wife's choice of a hus-
      band for Elizabeth.
    - _____ (c) That he approves of what Elizabeth has said to
      Mr. Collins.
    - _____ (d) That he does not approve of Elizabeth's choice of
      a husband.

TIME _____

SCORE _____

PART SEVEN

Reading the Whole Composition

You should now be ready to read some longer selections for speed and comprehension. If you have done the previous exercises conscientiously, you should have acquired efficient reading habits which will allow you to read the following selections rapidly yet without losing the meaning of what you are reading. Let us review once more some of the principles of good reading which you have already had an opportunity to practice.

1. Force yourself to read slightly faster than seems comfortable. Rapid reading will actually help you to concentrate better on ideas and the relations between ideas, for you will not have time to concern yourself with individual words.

2. As you read, try to get a sense of the writer's organization. Look for the *central ideas,* but do not neglect the supporting detail which the writer uses to reach his conclusions or support his argument.

3. Do not stop if you come to an unfamiliar word. Continue your reading, and it is very likely that the rest of the sentence (the "context") will make the meaning of the new word clear to you. (Occasionally in these selections you will be given footnotes to help you with hard words or phrases that are especially important for comprehension; however, do not bother to read the footnotes if you have a reasonably good idea what these words and phrases mean.)

4. Do not allow yourself to go back and reread words and phrases. Start with the idea that you will comprehend everything the first

time, and you will soon lose the habit of going back over parts of the material you have already read.

The three reading selections in this section are on very different subjects, but they are all of the same length—about 1000 words—and they are all of moderate difficulty. They represent typical kinds of material you might have to read in college courses, though they have been slightly simplified to enable you to read them fairly rapidly.

In doing each exercise, time yourself carefully as you read the selection, recording your time on the line marked TIME after the last line of the selection. Then go on to the Reading Comprehension Quiz that follows.

Noah Webster

The years during which the American colonies were fighting to establish their freedom from England produced an important change in their way of thinking. For many years the American settlers had depended on their mother country and had imported most of their books and many of their ideas from Europe. But having achieved political independence, many of the colonists began to develop a dislike for anything that seemed to suggest their former dependence. It became the fashion to demand an American civilization as different from that of Europe as were the political and social ideas which were being established in the New World.

No one expressed this attitude more strongly than Noah Webster (1758–1843). Born near Hartford, Connecticut, he received his education at Yale College and later began to practice law. But business in this profession was slow, and he was forced to turn to teaching. As a teacher, he soon discovered that the English schoolbooks then in use were unsatisfactory, and the American Revolution reduced the supply of such books as there were. Webster therefore began to work on three simple books on English, a spelling book, a grammar, and a reader, and these were the first books of their kind to be published in this country. The success of the first part was surprisingly great. It was soon issued again under the title *The American Spelling Book,* and in this form about 80 million copies were sold during the next hundred years. From a profit of less than one cent a copy, Webster got most of his income for the rest of his life. Not only did the little book have great influence on many generations of school children, but it also had the effect of turning its author's attention to questions of language. In 1806 he produced a small *Dictionary,* and this was followed by his greatest work, *An American Dictionary of the English Language,* published in two volumes in 1828. In both of these

The first four paragraphs are from *A History of the English Language,* 2nd Ed., by Albert C. Baugh. Copyright © 1957 by Appleton-Century-Crofts, Inc. Adapted by permission of Appleton-Century-Crofts, Inc. and the author.

works and in many smaller writings he had one purpose: to show that the English language in his country was a truly American thing, developing in its own special way and deserving to be considered from an independent, American point of view. As he himself wrote, "It is not only important, but in a degree necessary, that the people of this country should have an *American Dictionary* of the English language; for, although the body of the language is the same as in England . . . some differences exist. . . . The principal differences between the people of this country and of all others, arise from different forms of government, different laws, institutions and customs. . . . The institutions which are new and peculiar, give rise to new terms unknown to the people of England. . . . No person in this country will be satisfied with the English definitions of the words *congress, senate, assembly, court,* [and so forth] for although these are words used in England, yet they are applied in this country to express ideas which they do not express in that country." By giving American meanings and American pronunciation, by adopting a number of American spellings, and especially by introducing quotations from American authors beside those from English literature, he was able, to a great extent, to justify the title of his work. If, after a hundred years, some people still doubt the existence of a separate American language, his efforts, nevertheless, have left a lasting mark on the language of his country.

His influence on American spelling

It is a matter of common observation that American spelling is different, in small ways, from that which is usual in England. For example, Americans write words like *honor* and *color* without the *u* of English *honour* and *colour;* they write *er* instead of *re* in a number of words like *center* and *theater;* and they prefer an *s* to a *c* in words like *defense* and *offense.* The differences often pass unnoticed, partly because a number of English spellings are still current in America, partly because some of the American changes are now common in England, and partly because in many cases both an English and an American spelling of a word are common in both countries. Although some of the differences have arisen since Webster's day, most of the peculiarly American spellings are due to their occurrence in his dictionary.

His influence on American pronunciation

Though the influence is more difficult to prove, there can be no doubt that Webster is responsible for some of the characteristic features of American pronunciation, especially its uniformity and the way it tends to give fuller value to the unaccented syllables. Webster recommended that when pupils were learning to spell, they should pronounce each syllable of a word separately, and give proper attention to every letter in every syllable. When we consider that his *American Spelling Book* was used in thousands of schools over a great many years, it seems certain that considerable influence on American pronunciation is to be traced back to the little blue-covered spelling book.

His influence on later dictionaries

Two years after Webster brought out his dictionary of 1828, his lifelong rival Joseph Worcester published a smaller, cheap dictionary in which he borrowed freely from Webster. The Worcester dictionary, which soon became far more popular than those which Webster had produced, included many additional words, brief, clear definitions, full indication of pronunciation, the use of special marks to divide syllables, and lists of synonyms. In 1847, a few years after Webster's death, his son-in-law Chauncey Goodrich published a new dictionary under the Webster name. The years that followed saw a constant battle between the Webster and Worcester dictionaries, the battle finally being won by the Webster dictionary of 1864, from which most of the characteristics of Noah Webster were absent. The Webster dictionaries won the victory partly because the *American Spelling Book* had made the Webster name familiar all over America and partly because of the death of Worcester in 1865.

TIME_____*

---

* After you finish the rest of the exercise, consult the reading-time conversion table on pp. 177-78 to determine your *reading rate*.

Reading Comprehension Quiz

Directions: For each problem, put a check mark before the one choice (A, B, C, or D) which correctly completes the sentence or answers the question. *Do not look back at the reading selection in working these problems.*

1. Webster *first* tried to earn his living in the field of
   - _____ (a) education _____ (c) law
   - _____ (b) journalism _____ (d) medicine

2. Webster earned most of his money from the sale of his
   - _____ (a) dictionary of 1828 _____ (c) grammar
   - _____ (b) spelling book _____ (d) reader

3. Apparently Webster published his first books while he was a
   - _____ (a) teacher _____ (c) lawyer
   - _____ (b) student _____ (d) doctor

4. The author feels that Webster's influence on American pronunciation
   - _____ (a) was greater than his influence on spelling
   - _____ (b) is harder to prove than his influence on spelling
   - _____ (c) was not really as great as people commonly suppose
   - _____ (d) is the most important effect of his dictionary of 1828

5. Webster used the words *congress* and *senate* as examples of words which
   - _____ (a) had the same spelling in America and England
   - _____ (b) were pronounced differently in America and England
   - _____ (c) were developed in America, not in England
   - _____ (d) had different meanings in America and England

6. Worcester brought out his dictionary two years
   - _____ (a) before Webster published his
   - _____ (b) after Webster published his
   - _____ (c) before Webster's death
   - _____ (d) after Webster's death

7. As compared with Webster's dictionary of 1828, the first Worcester dictionary apparently was

_____ (a) larger and more expensive

_____ (b) smaller but more expensive

_____ (c) larger but less expensive

_____ (d) smaller and less expensive

8. According to the essay, which one of the following spellings would Webster most probably NOT have considered truly American?

_____ (a) *assembly*   _____ (c) *offence*

_____ (b) *honor*   _____ (d) *theater*

9. According to the essay, Chauncey Goodrich was

_____ (a) a relation of Worcester's

_____ (b) a relation of Webster's

_____ (c) a close friend of Worcester's

_____ (d) a rival of Webster's

10. According to the essay, the material in Worcester's first dictionary was

_____ (a) borrowed in large part from Webster

_____ (b) borrowed in large part from Goodrich

_____ (c) borrowed in large part from earlier books from England

_____ (d) almost entirely his own

SCORE_____

108

Professor Agassiz and the Fish

It was more than fifteen years ago that I entered the laboratory of Professor Agassiz and told him I had enrolled in the Scientific School as a student of natural history. He asked me a few questions about my purpose in coming, the manner in which I afterwards proposed to use the knowledge I might acquire, and finally whether I wished to study any special branch. To the last of these questions I replied that while I wished to obtain a sound knowledge of all aspects of zoology,[1] I planned to devote myself especially to insects.

"When do you wish to begin?" he asked.

"Now," I replied.

This seemed to please him, and with a quick "Very well!" he took down a huge jar of specimens in yellow alcohol.

"Take this fish," he said, "and look at it; we call it a haemulon; after a while I will ask you what you have seen."

With that he left me, but in a moment returned with specific instructions as to the care of the object entrusted to me. "No man is fit to be a naturalist," he said, "who does not know how to take care of specimens."

I was to keep the fish before me in a tin tray and occasionally moisten the surface with alcohol from the jar, always taking care to replace the top and fasten it tightly.

In ten minutes I had seen all that could be seen in that fish and started in search of the professor, who had, however, left the Museum, and when I returned, my specimen was dry all over. I dashed the fluid over the fish as if to revive the beast from a fainting attack and looked with anxiety for a return of its normal appearance. This little excitement over, nothing was to be done but to return to a steady gaze at my silent com-

---

[1] ZOOLOGY: the scientific study of animal life.

Adapted from "In the Laboratory with Agassiz" by Samuel Scudder, in *Every Saturday* (April 4, 1874).

panion. Half an hour passed—an hour—another hour; the fish began to look most unpleasant. I turned it over and around; looked at it in the face—horrible; from behind, beneath, above, sideways, at a three-quarters view—just as horrible. I was in despair; at an early hour I decided that lunch was necessary; so with infinite relief I carefully replaced the fish in the jar, and for an hour I was free.

On my return, I learned that Professor Agassiz had been at the Museum but had gone and would not return for several hours. My fellow students were too busy to be disturbed by continued conversation. Slowly I drew forth that ugly fish and with a feeling of desperation again looked at it. I pushed my finger down its throat to feel how sharp the teeth were. I began to count the scales in the different rows, until I was convinced that that was nonsense. At last a happy thought struck me: I would draw the fish. And now with surprise I began to discover new features in the creature. Just then the professor reurned. "That is right," he said; "a pencil is one of the best of eyes. I am glad to notice, too, that you keep your specimen wet and your bottle tightly closed." With these encouraging words he added: "Well, what is it like?"

He listened closely to my brief description of the structure of the parts whose names were still unknown to me. When I had finished, he waited as if expecting more, and then said disappointedly: "You have not looked very carefully; why," he continued more earnestly, "you haven't seen one of the most obvious features of the animal, which is as plainly before your eyes as the fish itself. Look again, look again!" And he left me to my misery.

Still more of that wretched fish! But now I set myself to my task with the greatest energy and discovered one new thing after another, until I saw how just the professor's criticism had been. The afternoon passed quickly, and then, toward its close, the professor returned and inquired: "Do you see it now?"

"No," I replied, "but I see how little I saw before."

"That is encouraging," he said earnestly, "but I won't hear you now; put away your fish and go home; perhaps you will be ready with a better answer in the morning. I will examine you before you look at the fish."

This was upsetting. Not only must I think of my fish all night, studying, without the object before me, what this unknown but most visible feature might be, but also without reviewing my discoveries I must give an exact account of them the next day. I had a bad memory; so I walked home by the Charles River in a confused state, with my two problems.

The cordial greeting of the professor the next morning was comforting; here was a man who seemed to be quite as anxious as I that I should see for myself what he saw.

"Do you perhaps mean," I asked, "that the fish has symmetrical sides with paired organs?" [2]

His pleased reply, "Of course, of course!" repaid the sleepless hours of the previous night. After he had talked with great enthusiasm for some time upon the importance ōf this point, I ventured to ask what I should do next.

"Oh, look at your fish!" he said and left me again. In a little more than an hour, he returned and heard my new account. "That is good, that is good!" he repeated, "but that is not all; go on." And so for three long days he placed that fish before my eyes, forbidding me to look at anything else. "Look, look, look" was his repeated command.

This was the best zoological lesson I ever had: a lesson whose influence has extended to the details of every later study, a gift the professor has left to me, as he has left it to many others, of the greatest value, which we could not buy, with which we cannot part.

TIME_____*

---

[2] SYMMETRICAL SIDES WITH PAIRED ORGANS: two sides exactly alike, with the organs in pairs, one on each side.

---

* After you finish the rest of the exercise, consult the reading-time conversion table on pp. 177-78 to determine your *reading rate*.

Reading Comprehension Quiz

Directions: For each problem, put a check mark before the one correct answer to the question. *Do not look back at the reading selection in working these problems.*

1. What kind of creatures did the writer especially wish to study?
   - _____ (a) birds
   - _____ (b) fish
   - _____ (c) snakes
   - _____ (d) insects

2. What directions did the professor give concerning the bottle of alcohol?
   - _____ (a) It had to be kept in a cool place.
   - _____ (b) It had to be kept tightly covered.
   - _____ (c) It had to be kept out of the sun.
   - _____ (d) It had to be kept completely full.

3. What happened to the fish when the writer first left it while he looked for the professor?
   - _____ (a) It became very soft.
   - _____ (b) It seemed to grow smaller.
   - _____ (c) It became completely dry.
   - _____ (d) It seemed to grow larger.

4. What was the professor's reaction to the writer's first description of the fish?
   - _____ (a) disappointment   _____ (c) delight
   - _____ (b) amusement   _____ (d) anger

5. What happened when the writer began to draw the fish?
   - _____ (a) He noticed many new things about it.
   - _____ (b) He found that he was unable to make it look natural.
   - _____ (c) He grew to hate it more and more.
   - _____ (d) He became angry with the professor.

6. How did the professor respond to the writer's drawing?
   _____ (a) He did not like the picture.
   _____ (b) He praised the writer's drawing ability.
   _____ (c) He approved of the idea of drawing the fish.
   _____ (d) He told the writer to use his eyes instead of a pencil.
7. How did the professor refer to the pencil?
   _____ (a) As "an unscientific tool."
   _____ (b) As "one of the best of eyes."
   _____ (c) As "the zoologist's best friend."
   _____ (d) As "a useless toy."
8. As he spent the afternoon with the fish, how did the writer come to feel about the professor?
   _____ (a) He could not understand the professor's purpose.
   _____ (b) He felt that the professor's method was cruel.
   _____ (c) He decided to take all his zoology work with the professor.
   _____ (d) He saw that the professor's criticism was just.
9. What did the writer have to do at night?
   _____ (a) Take the fish home and study it.
   _____ (b) Make another drawing of the fish.
   _____ (c) Think about the fish without seeing it.
   _____ (d) Learn the scientific names for the parts of the fish.
10. What obvious feature of the fish had the writer failed to notice?
   _____ (a) Its sharp teeth.
   _____ (b) Its unusual tail.
   _____ (c) Its arrangement of scales.
   _____ (d) Its symmetrical sides.

SCORE _____

EXERCISE 14

Scandinavian Influence on the English Vocabulary

In the year 787 began a series of events which were to have a great effect upon the history of the English language. For it was in that year, according to the records that have come down to us, that the Scandinavians made their first attack on the English coast. It is not known exactly why, after centuries of peace, the Scandinavians suddenly began their attacks on all the lands along the North Sea and the Baltic. But in the eighth century some development, perhaps economic and perhaps political, caused these people to leave their homes and seek adventure at sea. These daring sea-warriors are commonly known as Vikings, and the period of their great activity, commencing in the eighth century and extending to the beginning of the eleventh, is popularly called the Viking Age.

In the Viking attacks on England, three definite stages can be seen. The first, beginning in 787 and continuing with some interruptions until about 850, consisted simply of brief attacks on the English coast for the purpose of seizing gold, silver, and other valuables, and of carrying away slaves. These early raids were apparently the work of small, independent bands of men.

The second stage, from about 850 to 878, was the work of large armies and ended in extensive Viking settlements in England. It began in 850 with the arrival of a great Viking fleet near London, the city itself being captured the following year. After seizing large areas of the east, the Vikings proceeded to turn their attention to the south. The English king at this time was Alfred the Great. At first even the greatness of this king was insufficient to hold back the Viking armies, but in 878 Alfred, with fresh forces of men from the southern counties, suddenly attacked the Vikings and won an overwhelming victory. By the Treaty of Wedmore, signed by King Alfred and the leader of the Vikings in 878, the Vikings agreed to withdraw to the north and east of the country—though they were not forced to leave England altogether. In addition, the Vikings agreed to accept Christianity as their religion.

The third stage of the Scandinavian invasion of England covers the period from 878 to 1042. The Treaty of Wedmore by no means put an end to England's trouble with the Vikings. Periodically they renewed their attacks on the English, but under Alfred, and later under his son and then his grandson, the English were able to defend their lands against the enemy. Then, at the end of the tenth century, a powerful Viking fleet under Olaf Tryggvason and his friends began strong new attacks near London. Olaf was soon joined by Svein, the king of Denmark. In 1014 Svein drove the king of England from the country and seized the throne. Upon his sudden death the same year, he was followed by his son, Cnut. Three years of fighting left Cnut the undisputed king of England, and for the next twenty-five years (until 1042) England was ruled by Danish kings.

As a result of these events, large numbers of Scandinavians settled in England, becoming farmers and often marrying English women. Some idea of their numbers may be gained from the fact that more than 1400 places in England still have Scandinavian names. Most of the new inhabitants were Danes, though there were also considerable Norwegian settlements, particularly in the northwest.

With the gradual and peaceful union of Scandinavians and English, it was only natural that the two peoples would begin to borrow words from each other's language—the languages being quite similar to begin with. Indeed, because of this similarity it is often very difficult to determine whether a particular word in Modern English is a native or a borrowed word. And if we expect to find that the borrowed Scandinavian words fall into any special classes, we shall be disappointed. For the civilization of the Danes was very much like that of the English themselves, and so the words that were borrowed by the English tend to be of a simple, everyday character. Their varied nature can best be shown by a few examples. Among the nouns which English acquired from Scandinavian are *birth, dirt, egg, guess, kid, seat, skin, sky, want,* and *window.* The borrowed verbs include *call, die, get, give, lift, raise,* and *take.*

Quite obviously the words in the above lists do not represent new objects and ideas which the English received from the

116

Scandinavians. Rather, the Scandinavian and English words for these and many other everyday objects, actions, and ideas must have been used side by side for a while, and the survival of one or the other of them in English must often have been a mere matter of chance.

Altogether about nine hundred words in present-day Standard English are definitely known to have been borrowed from Scandinavian. And quite likely there are at least an equal number for which Scandinavian origin is probable or which show some Scandinavian influence. In addition, scholars tell us that thousands of Scandinavian words are still used in the everyday speech of the people who live in the north and east of England —words which have never entered the standard language but which have been handed down from generation to generation of English-speakers within certain regions of the country.

As for the hundreds upon hundreds of Scandinavian personal names and place names which have been taken into English, it is not possible in this brief survey to do more than give a few examples. To illustrate the former, we may refer to personal names ending in -son, such as *Johnson, Thompson,* and *Wilson.* Such names, showing a typical Scandinavian formation, appear as far back as the records of late Old English times. In similar fashion, English place names ending in -by, such as *Derby* and *Rugby,* clearly come to us from Scandinavian, where the ending signified a town or settlement.

TIME_____*

---

* After you finish the rest of the exercise, consult the reading-time conversion table on pp. 177-78 to determine your *reading rate.*

117

Reading Comprehension Quiz

Directions: For each problem, put a check mark before the one correct answer to the question. *Do not look back at the reading selection in working these problems.*

1. During what century did the Vikings make their first attacks upon England?

   _____ (a) the seventh   _____ (c) the ninth

   _____ (b) the eighth   _____ (d) the tenth

2. How does the author describe the Viking attacks of the *second* stage?

   _____ (a) They were carried out by small, independent bands of men.

   _____ (b) They were intended to recapture the territories given up to Alfred the Great.

   _____ (c) They were the work of large armies and ended in extensive settlements.

   _____ (d) They were brief raids for the purpose of seizing gold, silver, and slaves.

3. Who won the battle that led to the Treaty of Wedmore?

   _____ (a) Olaf   _____ (c) Alfred

   _____ (b) Svein   _____ (d) Cnut

4. For about how many years was England ruled by Danish kings?

   _____ (a) 15   _____ (c) 40

   _____ (b) 25   _____ (d) 55

5. Which of the following pairs of kings were father and son?

   _____ (a) Alfred and Svein   _____ (c) Svein and Cnut

   _____ (b) Olaf and Svein   _____ (d) Alfred and Cnut

6. What kind of words, in general, did the English borrow from the Scandinavians?

   _____ (a) Words for new objects and ideas.

   _____ (b) Words relating to war.

   _____ (c) Literary words.

   _____ (d) Simple, everyday words.

7. According to the writer, about how many words in present-day Standard English are definitely known to be Scandinavian borrowings?

_____ (a) 500   _____ (c) 1200

_____ (b) 900   _____ (d) 1500

8. Which one of the following place names clearly shows Scandinavian influence, as discussed in the essay?

_____ (a) Whitby   _____ (c) Hampshire

_____ (b) Winchester   _____ (d) Hampton

9. Which one of the following personal names shows "a typical Scandinavian formation" discussed in the essay?

_____ (a) Browning   _____ (c) Churchill

_____ (b) Spenser   _____ (d) Stevenson

10. According to the essay, when did the Viking Age come to an end?

_____ (a) During the first half of the eleventh century.

_____ (b) During the second half of the eleventh century.

_____ (c) During the first half of the twelfth century.

_____ (d) During the second half of the twelfth century.

SCORE _____

PART EIGHT

Reading to Locate Specific Information: Scanning

Sometimes our purpose in reading is simply to locate the answers to some very specific questions. For example, in the preparation of a research paper we may have to consult a number of reference books in order to find particular names, dates, figures, or definitions. We shall certainly not want to read these books with the same care that we would devote to an assigned chapter in a class textbook. Instead, our method will be to run our eyes rapidly over the material until we come to the place where the author discusses the particular matter that concerns us. Here we shall decrease our reading speed and read with care until we locate the specific item of information that we need. We shall probably not continue beyond that point, for we shall have fulfilled our special reading purpose.

The technique described above is called *scanning*, and, like other kinds of reading, it requires both special procedures and extensive practice if it is to become an efficient and automatic process.

The method of efficient scanning may be briefly summarized as follows:

1. Begin with a very clear understanding of what you are looking for. Limit your search to one or, at most, two items of information at a time.
2. Decide in advance what form the information is likely to take. If it is a person's name, you will want to look for initial capital letters. If it is the title of a book, you will be looking for italics.

If it is a date, you will look for figures. And if it is the description of an event, the discussion of an idea, the definition of a term, or the like, you should be looking for key words which would be likely to occur in such a description or discussion. For example, if you are reading a biography to find someone's occupation, you should look for words like *occupation, work, employment, livelihood,* and so forth.

3. Pass quickly over all material that is not directly related to the information you seek. Do not allow your attention to be diverted from your specific task, for otherwise you will slow down your speed and are even apt to forget your original purpose.

Now try to apply the above procedure in working the exercises that follow.

Exercise 15

Scanning Short Paragraphs

Directions: This exercise is designed to give you practice in scanning short passages of college-level English. You will be given ten paragraphs from reference works, textbooks, and similar material. Each paragraph is preceded by a very specific question together with five possible answers, only one of which is correct according to the paragraph. First read the question but do not bother to look at the five choices. When you have the question well in mind, scan the paragraph rapidly until you find the answer. Then return to the five choices and put a check mark before the one which you have found to be correct. Work as rapidly and as accurately as you can.

Question one:

Why is Mary Outerbridge important in the history of lawn tennis?

_____ (a) She invented it.
_____ (b) She gave it its name.
_____ (c) She introduced it to Bermuda.
_____ (d) She was the first American champion.
_____ (e) She brought it to the United States.

Paragraph one:

Lawn tennis is a comparatively modern sport, being based upon the ancient game of court tennis, which probably originated in Egypt or Persia some 2500 years ago. Major Walter Wingfield thought that something like court tennis could be played outdoors on lawns, and in December, 1873, he introduced his new game, which he called *Sphairistike,* at a lawn party in Wales. The sport became popular very rapidly, but the strange, awkward name disappeared almost at once, being replaced by the very simple and logical term "lawn tennis." By 1874 the game was being played by British soldiers in Bermuda, and in the early months of that year a young lady named Mary Outerbridge returned from Bermuda to New York, bringing with her the equipment necessary to play the new game. With the help of one of her brothers, she laid out a court on the grounds of the Staten Island Cricket and Baseball Club, and there, in the spring of 1874, Miss Outerbridge and some of her friends played the first game of lawn tennis in the United States. And just two years later, in 1876, the first United States lawn tennis tournament was held—at Nahant near Boston.

Question two:

When did Shakespeare buy his house in Stratford?

_____	(a)	1585
_____	(b)	1596
_____	(c)	1597
_____	(d)	1611
_____	(e)	1616

Paragraph two:

There has been much idle talk about Shakespeare's married life. The simple facts are that he left his wife at Stratford (their son, Hamnet, died and was buried there in 1596 and there is no evidence that Anne ever joined him during his stay in London), that no children were born to them after 1585, that about 1611 he moved his wife and children into New Place, the fine house in Stratford that he had purchased in 1597, and that he joined them there and died in that house in 1616.

Adapted from *Shakespeare: Twenty-Three Plays and the Sonnets* edited by Thomas Marc Parrott, 1953. Reprinted by permission of Charles Scribner's Sons.

Question three:

At what time of year does Louisiana have its minimum rainfall?

_____ (a) In winter.
_____ (b) In spring.
_____ (c) In summer.
_____ (d) In autumn.
_____ (e) The rate remains constant throughout the year.

Paragraph three:

The entire state of Louisiana is within a damp, subtropical zone. The average annual temperature of the state is 67° Fahrenheit, and monthly mean temperatures vary from 52° in January and December to 82° in July and August. The length of the growing season is usually between 220 and 250 days in the northern half of the state, and between 250 and 275 days in the southern half. The annual rainfall of the state averages about fifty-five inches, with a minimum in autumn. In the southern half the maximum is in summer, with frequent heavy thunderstorms; in the northern half the winter and spring rains exceed those of summer. Cane sugar is the principal product of the delta region; rice is grown in the prairies of southwestern Louisiana, and near the coast such subtropical fruits as oranges, olives, figs, and grapefruit are grown. Outside of these areas, cotton is the principal crop.

_____

Adapted from *Climatology: General and Regional* by Thomas A. Blair, 1957. Reprinted by permission of Prentice-Hall, Inc.

Question four:

What did Julius Caesar do to keep physicians in Rome?

_____ (a) He made them all Roman citizens.
_____ (b) He paid them all large sums of money.
_____ (c) He made them all slaves.
_____ (d) He built fine hospitals for them.
_____ (e) He gave them all high social rank.

Paragraph four:

During early Roman history all physicians were either slaves or representatives of lower Roman society. Medicine was a Greek science, and many Greek physicians, attracted by the prospect of great profits at the capital of the empire, migrated to Rome to establish their practice. As a consequence, many doctors were foreigners, and as such were considered in a very low position by the people of high social rank. Frequently, a wealthy Roman supplied one of his slaves with a medical education for the sake of convenience. Having one's own physician was obviously an advantage not to be overlooked, and slaves who had a knowledge of the healing art commanded the highest prices in the Roman slave market. Recognizing the importance of the medical profession, however, Julius Caesar conferred citizenship on all who practiced medicine at Rome to make them more desirous of living in the city, and to induce others to come to it. Despite this encouragement, medicine never came to be considered the proper profession for the upper classes.

Adapted from "Medical Practice in Ancient Rome (1-125 A.D.)" by Hall Tacket, in *Complete College Composition*, 2nd Ed., edited by A. Wigfall Green, Dudley R. Hutcherson, William B. Leake, and Pete Kyle McCartner. Copyright 1940, 1945 by F. S. Crofts and Company. Reprinted by permission of Appleton-Century-Crofts, Inc.

Question five:

What was Walt Whitman's occupation after he moved to New Orleans?

_____ (a) teacher
_____ (b) printer
_____ (c) bus driver
_____ (d) newspaper writer
_____ (e) sailor

Paragraph five:

Walt Whitman was born May 31, 1819, on Long Island, New York, of a family of workers. His ancestors had been mainly farmers, but his father turned carpenter and moved his family to Brooklyn, New York. Here the country child became a town boy. He roamed about the docks, explored the alleys, loved the sharp wood-smell of his father's shop and the exciting noises of the street. At eleven young Whitman went to work as an errand boy. At twelve he learned to set type, and at fourteen he went to work as a printer for a Long Island newspaper. For the next twenty years he earned a living as printer, reporter, and occasional teacher. He wrote short and sentimental pieces, harmless verses, and undistinguished editorials for forgotten newspapers. In his thirtieth year Whitman left New York for New Orleans, to become a special writer on the staff of a newspaper. Then, at thirty-one, he ceased to write polite sketches and began to fashion a rough and spacious poetry. He exchanged his well-tailored suit for the clothes of a workman and associated with sailors, bus drivers, and other uneducated persons. He became aware of, and learned to love, the rich and powerful sounds of the American language.

Adapted from *A Treasury of Great Poems, English and American* edited by Louis Untermeyer, 1942. Reprinted by permission of Simon and Schuster, Inc.

Name _____

How did Amherst College get its name?

_____ (a) From one of the founders of the College.
_____ (b) From the place where the College is located.
_____ (c) From a poet who lived near the College.
_____ (d) From a citizen who gave the College money.
_____ (e) From the first president of the College.

Paragraph six:

    Since its beginning in 1821, Amherst has been an independent liberal arts college. Amherst has never associated formally with any church or sect. Its charter, granted by the Commonwealth of Massachusetts in 1825, simply commits the College to "the education of youth" and forbids tests of religion in choosing students or faculty. Founded by men like Noah Webster and Samuel Fowler Dickinson, grandfather of the poet Emily Dickinson, Amherst received its initial support from many citizens of the town from which it takes its name. It has had a long association with the surrounding community, particularly with such poets and writers as Emily Dickinson, Helen Hunt Jackson, David Grayson, and Robert Frost. But the College is also associated with universal traditions of scholarship and learning. Its faculty holds degrees from institutions of higher learning all over the world, and its students come from all parts of the United States and many foreign countries.

Question seven:

What was the importance of the "Kalamazoo Case" in the history of United States education?

_____ (a) Free public education became available beyond the elementary school.

_____ (b) Private academies were established to provide secondary education.

_____ (c) An elementary education for all children became a requirement by law.

_____ (d) A secondary education for all children became a requirement by law.

_____ (e) The first free college was established in the United States.

Paragraph seven:

Until about 1850 the common elementary school was considered adequate for the education of the large majority of children in the United States. Secondary schools, starting with the establishment of Benjamin Franklin's Academy in Philadelphia a hundred years earlier, were mostly private or at least were financed by private funds. The establishment of the first public high school in 1821 marked the beginning of the upward extension of the tax-supported schools. In 1872 the decision of the Michigan Supreme Court in what is known as the "Kalamazoo Case" established that communities could tax themselves to provide educational activities beyond the elementary school. Previously the academies had satisfied the desire for continued education and preparation for college— at least for those who were willing to pay for it. The high schools now were to provide such education at public expense; and their success was indicated, at least in part, by their rapid growth after 1890.

Adapted from the *Encyclopedia of Educational Research* edited by Chester W. Harris. Copyright © 1960 by the *American Educational Research Association*. Reprinted by permission of The Macmillan Company.

Question eight:

By what date had printed books almost completely replaced hand-written books in England?

_____ (a) 1450
_____ (b) 1476
_____ (c) 1500
_____ (d) 1526
_____ (e) 1576

Paragraph eight:

The invention of the process of printing from movable type, which occurred in Germany about the middle of the fifteenth century, was destined to exercise a far-reaching influence on all the living languages of Europe. Introduced into England about 1476 by William Caxton, who had learned the art on the continent, printing made such rapid progress that a mere century later it was observed that handwritten books were seldom to be met with and almost never used. Some idea of the rapidity with which the new process swept forward may be had from the fact that in Europe the number of books printed before the year 1500 reaches the surprising figure of 35,000. The majority of these, it is true, were in Latin, whereas it is in the modern languages that the effect of the printing press was chiefly to be felt. But in England over 20,000 titles in English had appeared by 1640, ranging all the way from small pamphlets to huge volumes. The result was to bring books, which had formerly been the expensive luxury of the few, within the reach of all.

Adapted from *A History of the English Language*, 2nd Ed., by Albert C. Baugh. Copyright © 1957 by Appleton-Century-Crofts, Inc. Reprinted by permission of Appleton-Century-Crofts, Inc. and the author.

Question nine:

What event of the American Revolution persuaded France to aid the American colonies?

_____ (a) The surrender of Cornwallis.
_____ (b) The Battle of Saratoga.
_____ (c) The visit of Franklin to Paris.
_____ (d) The British capture of New York.
_____ (e) The issuing of the Declaration of Independence.

Paragraph nine:

The American Revolution began in New England, with battles at Lexington, Concord, Bunker Hill and elsewhere near Boston. The English troops won most of the engagements but, finding themselves in an unfriendly region far from their base of supplies, finally evacuated the city. Meanwhile, representatives of the American colonies had met in the First and Second Continental Congresses, and the latter body functioned as a government during most of the war. It issued the Declaration of Independence on July 4, 1776, declaring the colonies free of British rule. After the fighting around Boston had ended, the British then captured New York by driving out the smaller American force under George Washington. But they suffered a great disaster when an army under Burgoyne was captured at Saratoga in October, 1777. The battle proved itself a decisive engagement, since it convinced France that the colonies could win their independence and thus brought French aid. Benjamin Franklin, who had already gone to Paris in search of such aid, was now able to sign treaties of commerce and alliance. The British next transferred the war to the southern colonies. There they won many battles, but finally their army under General Cornwallis was trapped by a combined French and American force by land and a French fleet at sea. The surrender of Cornwallis virtually ended the war.

Adapted from *History of England* by J. A. Rickard, 1953. Reprinted by permission of Barnes & Noble, Inc.

Question ten:

Why was Noah Webster's dictionary of 1828 not a general success?

_____ (a) It was too much like Dr. Johnson's.
_____ (b) It was too inferior to Walker's.
_____ (c) It was too large and expensive.
_____ (d) It was written in too difficult a style.
_____ (e) It was too poorly printed and illustrated.

Paragraph ten:

The earliest American dictionaries were simple little school-books based chiefly on the famous dictionary of the Englishman Samuel Johnson. The first important date in American dictionary making is 1828, the year that Noah Webster published *An American Dictionary of the English Language,* in two volumes. Webster's book has many weaknesses (such as a crude pronunciation system actually inferior to that of Walker's dictionary of 1791), but in its insistence upon American spellings, in definitions keyed to the American scene, and in its illustrative quotations from the founders of the Republic, it provided the country with the first native dictionary comparable in scope to that of Dr. Johnson. Yet because of its two-volume size and its relatively high price it never achieved any great degree of popular acceptance in Webster's own lifetime. Probably its greatest contribution to later American dictionaries was in its style of definition writing--writing of a clarity and compactness never approached before its day.

TIME _____

SCORE _____

Exercise 16

Scanning an Article

Directions: In this scanning exercise, one long article is divided into five sections. At the beginning of each section you are given two questions. After you read the pair of questions, begin scanning the section to find the answers. When you find the answer to the first of the two questions, *draw a line* under the words that make up that answer. Then continue your scanning until you have answered the second question in the same way. Try to work rapidly but accurately.

Example:

1. In what century did the junior college movement have its beginnings?
2. How many junior colleges are under private control?

The junior college movement is a significant development in American higher education. The junior college, usually offering two years of education above the secondary school, is a product of the 20th century, with its greatest growth since 1940. The enrollment in the recognized junior colleges of the country has increased rapidly in recent years. There are now some 585 junior colleges, 330 under public control and 255 under private control.

The answer to the first question occurs in the fourth line—*20th century.* The answer to the second question is given in the last sentence—*255.* See how the answers have been underlined. Now turn the page and answer the five pairs of questions in the same manner.

145

Name _____

1. How many of the Colonial colleges were *not* founded by religious organizations?
2. What is the present name of King's College?

The American college dates back to Colonial times. The earliest one was Harvard College, established in 1636. Nine such institutions were founded before 1776. All but one of them were established by churches. They were patterned after the British colleges of Oxford and Cambridge Universities, but it should be noted that the independent college, not the university, was the model followed in the early period of American history. The purpose of the early colleges was to provide young men with a cultural background and to prepare them in a general way for practice in the professions, particularly in the Christian ministry.

After the Revolutionary War the functions of the higher-education institutions were extended and became more varied. Harvard College was mentioned in the constitution of Massachusetts adopted in 1780 as "The University at Cambridge." The College and Academy at Philadelphia, founded in 1755, became the University of Pennsylvania in 1791. The name of the College of Rhode Island, established in 1765, was changed to Brown University in 1804. Several of the earlier institutions continued in name as colleges long after they came to operate as universities. Thus the College of New Jersey (1746) was not formally known as Princeton University until 1896, and King's College, which was founded in 1754 and took the name of Columbia College in 1784, did not officially become Columbia University until 1912.

Adapted from *American Universities and Colleges,* 8th Ed., edited by Mary Irwin. Copyright 1960 by the American Council on Education. Reprinted by permission of the American Council on Education.

Two

3. How many permanent colleges were established before the Civil War?

4. What is the oldest institution of higher education west of the Mississippi River?

The period from 1780 to the Civil War was marked by a tremendous increase in the number of higher-education institutions, the rise of the state university, the creation of scientific and technological schools and departments, and the beginning of higher education for women.

Graduates of the Colonial colleges and leaders of the churches followed the American frontier westward, establishing colleges like those in the East. No fewer than 16 colleges were founded by Yale graduates before the Civil War, and Princeton claims that 25 colleges indirectly owe their existence to the efforts of its graduates. Of the 182 permanent colleges founded before the Civil War, 17 were in Ohio, 16 in Pennsylvania, and 15 in New York. West of the Mississippi River the first permanent colleges founded were St. Louis University, 1818, and the College of Louisiana (now called Centenary College), 1825; in the Northwest, Willamette University, Oregon, 1842; and in the Southwest, California Wesleyan College (now College of the Pacific), 1851.

Three

5. What kind of university did George Washington wish to see established?
6. What contribution did many of the early state universities receive from the federal government?

During the latter part of the nineteenth century, influenced by European universities, especially those in Germany, and compelled by the needs of American communities, the colleges began to liberalize their programs of study. The free elective principle, modern languages and the sciences, specialization and professional training, and individual responsibility for conduct were introduced by a number of colleges. At the same time the religious character of the institutions became less pronounced.

Among the early universities which were state-controlled or received state assistance were the University of Georgia, founded in 1785, the University of North Carolina, founded in 1789, and the University of Vermont, founded in 1791; others rapidly followed. Although the desire of a number of leaders of the day, including George Washington, for a national university was never realized, many of the 21 state universities established before the Civil War were aided by grants of land from the federal government. A number of the earlier state universities were subjected to some measure of private control, but by the middle of the nineteenth century full state control began to be widely assumed. Today each state maintains and controls one or more universities. The State of Pennsylvania supports but does not control the Pennsylvania State University and gives some financial assistance to three privately controlled universities. The State of New York in 1948 established the State University of New York, which is composed of 28 institutions of higher education situated at different places in the state.

Four

7. How many municipal universities are there?
8. Which university has the oldest program in law?

A second type of public institution of higher education is the municipal (city) university or college, which is controlled by municipal authorities and supported in part through city taxes. Some of these institutions were established under private control and later taken over by the municipalities; others were originally established under municipal control. Louisville College, founded by the city council in 1837, became the University of Louisville in 1846. The present City College had its origin in the Free Academy which was opened in New York City in 1849. The name was changed to the College of the City of New York in 1866, to the City College of New York in 1929, and in recent years to The City College. Cincinnati College (1819) became a municipal institution in 1870 and was renamed the University of Cincinnati. The largest of the municipal universities, of which there are 13, is The City College, with an enrollment of about 30,000.

The first professional instruction, other than in religion, which was offered in colleges and universities in the United States, was in medicine at the College, Academy, and Charitable School of Philadelphia (now University of Pennsylvania) in 1765. The first law school in the United States was conducted at Litchfield, Connecticut, from 1784 to 1833, and the first permanent instruction in the subject in the universities came with the establishment of the law faculty of the University of Maryland in 1816, and the law school at Harvard in 1817.

Name _____

Five

9. What is the name of the women's college at Tulane University?
10. How many states maintain separate colleges for women?

Between 1825 and 1875 the idea of college education for women developed in several sections of the country. At first it was provided in separate colleges for women, but when Oberlin Collegiate Institute (later Oberlin College) was opened in 1833 it admitted both men and women, the first degree-granting college to do so. For some years after the Civil War a number of separate colleges for women were established, but the trend was toward coeducation. The coordinate college, separately organized for women but operating parallel with a college for men, was established in several places. Examples are Radcliffe College of Harvard, Barnard College of Columbia University, and Newcomb College of Tulane University.

The state universities early opened their doors to women, and today all of them admit women to all or some parts of the institution. Eight southern states—Alabama, Georgia, Mississippi, North Carolina, Oklahoma, South Carolina, Texas, and Virginia—also maintain separate colleges for women. Only three of these—South Carolina, Texas, and Virginia—maintain institutions, usually technological or other specialized institutions, for men only.

SCORE _____

TIME _____

PART NINE

Using the Dictionary

In all the previous reading exercises in this book, you were advised not to stop reading when you came to an unfamiliar word, but to continue reading in the likelihood that the rest of the sentence (the "context") would make the meaning of the new word clear to you. This was sound advice in a book whose main purpose is to increase your general reading speed and efficiency. And certainly it is true that after we have acquired a basic vocabulary in a new language and have learned to read fairly fluently, we learn most new words from the contexts in which they occur.

At the same time, we do not mean to suggest that you should not make use of the dictionary in your reading. A dictionary is a most valuable tool for any serious reader, particularly when he is reading textbooks, reference works, or other materials containing technical language or other difficult kinds of vocabulary. And as you know from your past experience with dictionaries—particularly the larger college and unabridged types—they can provide you with many useful kinds of information in addition to the meanings of words.

Using the dictionary efficiently is just as dependent upon practice and good habits as are other kinds of reading. The exercises in this concluding section have therefore been designed to give you practice in using an English dictionary with greater speed and accuracy.

Finding Information in the Dictionary

Directions: In this exercise you are given a page from an American college dictionary, followed by a series of problems relating to the entries on that page. Read each problem rapidly and then consult the dictionary page to find the information that is asked for. Then return to the problem and put a check mark before the one choice that correctly completes the sentence or answers the question. Work as rapidly and as accurately as you can.

har·mon·i·ca (här-mon′i-kə), *n.* [L., fem. of *harmonicus*; see HARMONIC], 1. a musical instrument consisting of a series of graduated glasses from which tones are produced by rubbing the edges with a wet finger: invented by Benjamin Franklin. 2. a percussion instrument consisting of metal or glass strips which are struck with small mallets. 3. a small wind instrument played with the mouth: it has a series of graduated metal reeds that vibrate and produce tones when air is blown or sucked across them: also called *mouth organ.*

HARMONICA (sense 3)

har·mon·i·cal·ly (här-mon′i-k′l-i), *adv.* 1. [Archaic], harmoniously. 2. in *mathematics*, in a harmonic relation. 3. in *music*, with reference to harmony.

har·mon·i·con (här-mon′i-kən), *n. pl.* HARMONICA (-kə), [Gr. *harmonikon*, neut. of *harmonikos*; see HARMONIC], 1. a harmonica. 2. a barrel organ in which the tones of various instruments are imitated; orchestrion.

har·mon·ics (här-mon′iks), *n.pl.* [construed as sing.], [< *harmonic*], the science of musical sounds.

har·mo·ni·ous (här-mō′ni-əs), *adj.* [Fr. *harmonieux*; see HARMONY], 1. having parts combined in a proportionate, orderly, or pleasing arrangement; congruous. 2. having similar or conforming feelings, ideas, interests, etc.; in accord. 3. in *music*, having tones combined to give a pleasing effect; consonant.

har·mo·nist (här′mə-nist), *n.* 1. a musician or composer; especially, an expert in harmony. 2. a poet. 3. a literary scholar who arranges parallel passages of different authors, as in the Scriptures, so as to bring out corresponding ideas, qualities, etc. 4. a person who harmonizes something.

har·mo·ni·um (här-mō′ni-əm), *n.* [Fr. < L. *harmonia*; see HARMONY], a small keyboard organ in which the tones are produced by forcing air through metal reeds by means of a bellows operated by pedals.

har·mon·i·za·tion (här′mən-i-zā′shən, här′mən-ī-zā′-shən), *n.* a harmonizing or being harmonized.

har·mo·nize (här′mə-nīz′), *v.i.* [HARMONIZED (-nīzd′), HARMONIZING], [Fr. *harmoniser* < *harmonie*], to be, sing, or play in harmony; accord; agree. *v.t.* 1. to make harmonious; bring into agreement. 2. to add chords to (a melody) so as to form a harmony. —*SYN.* see **agree**.

har·mo·ny (här′mə-ni), *n.* [pl. HARMONIES (-niz)], [Fr. *harmonie*; L. *harmonia*; Gr. *harmonia* < *harmos*, a fitting, *harmozein*, to fit together], 1. a combination of parts into a proportionate or orderly whole; congruity. 2. agreement in feeling, action, ideas, interests, etc.; peaceable or friendly relations. 3. agreement or proportionate arrangement of color, size, shape, etc. that is pleasing to the eye; a fitting well together. 4. an arrangement of parallel passages of different authors, the Scriptures, etc., made so as to bring out corresponding ideas, qualities, etc. 5. agreeable sounds; music. 6. in *music*, a) the pleasing combination of two or more tones in a chord. b) structure in terms of the arrangement, progression, modulation, etc. of chords: distinguished from *melody, rhythm.* c) the study of this structure. —*SYN.* see **symmetry**.

har·ness (här′nis), *n.* [ME. *harneis*; OFr. *harneis, herneis, harnes*, armor], 1. originally, armor and other military equipment for a man or horse. 2. the leather straps and metal pieces by which a horse, mule, etc. is fastened to a vehicle, plow, or load. 3. any trappings or gear similar to this; specifically, a) the straps, etc. by which a parachute is fastened to its wearer. b) a device for raising and lowering the warp threads on a loom. *v.t.* 1. to put harness on (a horse, etc.). 2. to bring into a condition for working or producing power; as, the *harnessed* the power of the water by building a dam. 3. [Archaic], to put armor on.

in double harness, 1. in a harness for two animals pulling the same carriage, plow, etc. 2. married.

in harness, in or at one's routine work.

har·nessed antelope (här′nist), any of several striped African antelopes, as the bushbuck.

harness hitch, a kind of knot: see **knot**, illus.

Har·ney Peak (här′ni), the highest mountain of the

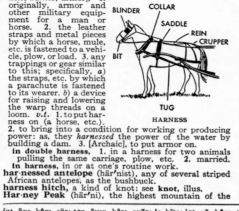

BLINDER COLLAR
SADDLE
REIN
CRUPPER
BIT
TUG

HARNESS

Black Hills, western South Dakota: height, 7,242 ft.

Har·old (har′əld), [AS. *Harold, Harald*; ON. *Haraldr*; Gmc. **Hariwald*, lit., ruler, leader of the army < **harja-*, army, host (AS. *here*) + **waldan*, to rule (cf. WIELD)], a masculine name: diminutive, *Hal.*

Harold I, ?–1040; son of Canute II; king of England (1035–1040): called *Harold Harefoot.*

Harold II, 1022?–1066; last Saxon king of England (1066); killed in the Battle of Hastings.

harp (härp), *n.* [ME. *herpe, harpe*; AS. *hearpe*; akin to G. *harfe*; IE. base*(s) *gereb(h)-*, to bend, curve, seen also in Norw. dial. *hurpa*, old, bent crone; the name comes from the shape of the instrument], 1. a musical instrument with strings stretched across an open, triangular frame, played by being plucked with the fingers: the modern harp has forty-six strings and a series of foot pedals which permit the playing of half tones. 2. a harp-shaped object or implement. 3. [H-], Lyra, a northern constellation. 4. [Slang], an Irishman: a vulgar term of prejudice and contempt. *v.i.* 1. to play a harp. 2. to persist in talking or writing tediously or continuously (*on* or *upon* something). *v.t.* [Rare], to give voice to; express.

HARP

Har·pers Ferry, Har·per's Ferry (här′pĕrz), a town in West Virginia, at the juncture of the Potomac and Shenandoah Rivers: site of John Brown's raid in 1859.

harp·ings (här′piŋz), *n.pl.* [prob. < Fr. *harper*, to grip], 1. wooden strips or planks on the bow of a ship to give it added strength. 2. wooden pieces used as supports during the construction of a ship.

harp·ins (här′piŋz), *n.pl.* harpings.

harp·ist (här′pist), *n.* a person who plays the harp.

har·poon (här-pōōn′), *n.* [Fr. *harpon*, dim. < *harpe*, a claw, or < MFr. *harper*, to claw, grip < Gmc. **harpan*, to seize], a barbed javelin or spear with a line attached to it, used for spearing whales or other large sea animals. *v.t.* to strike, kill, or catch with a harpoon.

harp·si·chord (härp′si-kôrd′), *n.* [obs. Fr. *harpechorde*; *harpe* (LL. *harpa*; Gmc. *harpa*; see HARP) + *chorde* (see CORD) -*s*- is unexplained], a stringed musical instrument with a keyboard, forerunner of the piano: it somewhat resembles the clavichord, except that when the keys are pressed the strings are plucked by leather-tipped points rather than struck by hammers, and produce short, abrupt tones.

HARPSICHORD

Har·py (här′pi), *n.* [pl. HARPIES (-piz)], [OFr. *harpie*; L. *harpyia*; Gr. *harpyiai*, pl., lit., snatchers < *harpazein*, to seize, snatch], 1. in *Greek mythology*, any of several hideous, filthy, winged monsters with the head and trunk of a woman and the tail, legs, and talons of a bird: they carried off the souls of the dead, seized the food of their victims, etc. 2. [h-], a relentless, greedy, or grasping person. 3. [h-], a harpy eagle.

harpy eagle, a large, short-winged, tropical American eagle, with a double crest and a powerful bill and claws.

har·que·bus (här′kwi-bəs), *n.* an arquebus, an early type of firearm.

Har·rar (hä′rĕr), *n.* Harar.

har·ri·dan (har′i-dən), *n.* [prob. altered < OFr. *haridelle*, worn-out horse, jade], a haggard, disreputable, shrewish old woman.

har·ri·er (har′i-ĕr), *n.* [< *hare* + *-ier*], 1. any of an English breed of dog, used for hunting hares and rabbits. 2. pl. the harriers and hunters in a hunt. 3. a cross-country runner.

har·ri·er (har′i-ĕr), *n.* 1. a person who harries. 2. a hawk that preys on insects and small animals.

Har·ri·et (har′i-ət), [fem. dim. of *Harry*], a feminine name: variants, *Harriot, Harriott*; diminutive, *Hattie.*

Har·ri·man, Edward Henry (har′i-mən), 1848–1909; American capitalist; railroad magnate.

Har·ris, Joel Chandler (chand′lĕr här′is), 1848–1908; American writer; wrote the *Uncle Remus* stories.

Har·ris·burg (har′is-bŭrg′), *n.* the capital of Pennsylvania, on the Susquehanna: pop., 89,000.

Har·ri·son, Benjamin (har′ə-s′n), 1. 1726?–1791;

1. If you were dividing the word *harmonica* in writing, which one of the following divisions would be acceptable?
   _____ (a) harm-onica _____ (c) harmon-ica
   _____ (b) harmo-nica _____ (d) harmonic-a

2. For his harmonica, Benjamin Franklin used a series of
   _____ (a) metal strips _____ (c) metal reeds
   _____ (b) glasses _____ (d) glass strips

3. The term *Harpy* or *harpy* is NOT applied to a kind of
   _____ (a) monster _____ (c) person
   _____ (b) bird _____ (d) dog

4. The name *Harold* means
   _____ (a) "judge of men"
   _____ (b) "ancient leader"
   _____ (c) "ruler of the army"
   _____ (d) "elder hero"

5. For a picture of a harness hitch, you would have to look
   _____ (a) on the previous page
   _____ (b) on the following page
   _____ (c) under *hitch*
   _____ (d) under *knot*

6. A further definition of harmony could be found by looking up
   _____ (a) *music* _____ (c) *rhythm*
   _____ (b) *melody* _____ (d) *symmetry*

7. *Harriet* is the feminine form of
   _____ (a) *Harry* _____ (c) *Harvey*
   _____ (b) *Harold* _____ (d) *Harriot*

8. On this page can be found the population of
   _____ (a) Harney Peak _____ (c) Harrisburg
   _____ (b) Harpers Ferry _____ (d) Harrar

9. Apparently the *original* harness was frequently worn by
   _____ (a) farmers _____ (c) ladies
   _____ (b) soldiers _____ (d) children

10. Which one of the following is NOT listed as a verb as well as a noun?
   _____ (a) *harp* _____ (c) *harpoon*
   _____ (b) *harness* _____ (d) *harrier*

11. Which of the following pairs of words are apparently never used to refer to the same thing?

_____ (a) *harmonica : harmonicon*

_____ (b) *harquebus : arquebus*

_____ (c) *harpins : harpings*

_____ (d) *harmonium : harmonicon*

12. Unlike the harpsichord, the clavichord has

_____ (a) keys

_____ (b) leather-tipped points

_____ (c) hammers

_____ (d) short strings

13. According to the dictionary, which one of the following meanings is no longer in use?

_____ (a) *harmonist:* "an expert in harmony"

_____ (b) *harmonize:* "to add chords to a melody"

_____ (c) *harmony:* "an arrangement of parallel passages"

_____ (d) *harmonically:* "harmoniously"

14. The dictionary does NOT print a plural form for

_____ (a) *Harpy*   _____ (c) *harmonium*

_____ (b) *harmony*   _____ (d) *harmonicon*

15. "They're in double harness" would most probably be said of

_____ (a) people who are doing two jobs at once

_____ (b) a husband and wife

_____ (c) people who are traveling together

_____ (d) a pair of twins

16. When *Harp* is capitalized, it refers to

_____ (a) a northern constellation

_____ (b) a harp-shaped instrument

_____ (c) an old, bent crone

_____ (d) an instrument with forty-six strings

17. The explanation of *Harrar* is to be found

_____ (a) at the bottom of this page

_____ (b) earlier under the letter *H*

_____ (c) later under the letter *H*

_____ (d) under the letter *A*

18. The harp was named for its

_____ (a) inventor   _____ (c) shape

_____ (b) sound   _____ (d) weight

162

19. The term *harrier* is apparently NOT applied to a kind of
_____ (a) person   _____ (c) fish
_____ (b) dog   _____ (d) hawk
20. Apparently scholars are not sure of the year that
_____ (a) Harold the First died
_____ (b) Edward Henry Harriman was born
_____ (c) Benjamin Harrison died
_____ (d) Harold the Second was born

TIME _____

SCORE _____

Exercise 18

"Catchwords"

Directions: "Catchwords" are the words which appear at the very top of each page of the dictionary to indicate the range of words on that page. The catchword above the left-hand column indicates the first entry on the page; the catchword on the right shows the last entry on the page.

fractional	574	France

In the above example we see that page 574 contains entries for all words from *fractional* to *France.* If, for instance, we were looking up the word *fragment,* we would know from the catchwords that it was on page 574.

In each of the two parts of this exercise you will first be given fifteen or sixteen sets of catchwords and page numbers. You will then find a series of words which would occur within the range of the dictionary pages you have been given. Decide on which page each word would occur, and write the number after the word.

These exercises are designed not only to increase your facility in using catchwords but also to give you practice in reacting quickly to the order of the letters in the alphabet. Work as rapidly and as accurately as you can. When you have finished Part One, go on to Part Two. Do not stop until you have completed both parts.

Name _____

catchwords and pages:

obituary	900	oblivious
oblong	901	observe
observer	902	occasion
occasional	903	occurrence
ocean	904	octopod
octopus	905	odorless
odorous	906	offend
offense	907	offset
offshoot	908	oily
ointment	909	old lady
Old Latin	910	Olympia
Olympian	911	on
onager	912	onset
onshore	913	open-air
open-and-shut	914	operation
operative	915	opponent

problems:

Directions: Indicate the page on which each of these words would be found.

Example:

omen   911   [between *Olympian* and *on*]

1. offence	_____	11. Olympic	_____
2. opening	_____	12. occult	_____
3. O.K.	_____	13. offspring	_____
4. occupy	_____	14. onus	_____
5. onlooker	_____	15. odour	_____
6. oboe	_____	16. observance	_____
7. objective	_____	17. operculum	_____
8. operatic	_____	18. old-time	_____
9. oblate	_____	19. opal	_____
10. office	_____	20. obsolete	_____

Two

catchwords and pages:

satisfy	1300	savant
save	1301	savoy
saw	1302	scads
scaffold	1303	scalp
scalpel	1304	scant
scantily	1305	Scarlatti
scarlet	1306	scenery
scenic	1307	scheme
scheming	1308	schnapps
schnauzer	1309	schoolmaster
schoolmate	1310	scissor
scissors	1311	scone
scoop	1312	scorn
scornful	1313	scow
scowl	1314	scratchy

problems:

Directions: Indicate the page on which each of these words would be found.

1. scamp _____
2. saxophone _____
3. scald _____
4. Schlegel _____
5. savor _____
6. schoolboy _____
7. scanty _____
8. scoff _____
9. sauce _____
10. scent _____

11. scimitar _____
12. scavenger _____
13. scorch _____
14. scene _____
15. scotch _____
16. scat _____
17. Schiller _____
18. scope _____
19. Savannah _____
20. scaup _____

TIME _____

SCORE _____

Key to the Exercises

Exercise one

1. c	11. b	21. a	31. d	41. d	51. a	61. c
2. c	12. b	22. b	32. b	42. a	52. a	62. a
3. a	13. a	23. d	33. d	43. a	53. d	63. b
4. d	14. d	24. c	34. c	44. b	54. c	64. c
5. a	15. b	25. a	35. d	45. c	55. c	65. c
6. b	16. d	26. d	36. d	46. b	56. b	
7. d	17. a	27. c	37. b	47. d	57. d	
8. c	18. a	28. b	38. b	48. b	58. c	
9. a	19. c	29. a	39. a	49. c	59. b	
10. c	20. d	30. c	40. b	50. b	60. d	

Exercise two

1. c	6. a
2. c	7. c
3. d	8. d
4. b	9. a
5. d	10. b

Exercise three

Score by inspection.

Exercise four

Score by inspection.

Exercise five

1. D	11. S	21. S	31. S	41. D	51. S
2. S	12. D	22. S	32. D	42. S	52. D
3. S	13. D	23. D	33. D	43. D	53. S
4. D	14. D	24. D	34. S	44. S	54. D
5. S	15. S	25. S	35. S	45. S	55. D
6. D	16. S	26. D	36. D	46. D	56. S
7. D	17. D	27. D	37. S	47. S	57. D
8. S	18. S	28. D	38. D	48. D	58. S
9. D	19. D	29. S	39. D	49. S	59. D
10. S	20. D	30. D	40. S	50. D	60. D

Exercise six

1. talk	11. reply	21. boat	31. surely	41. sound
2. seat	12. easy	22. get	32. find	42. still
3. start	13. big	23. fast	33. boy	43. suppose
4. close	14. funny	24. complete	34. like	44. town
5. get	15. work	25. raise	35. happen	45. whole
6. stay	16. hit	26. under	36. help	46. freedom
7. allow	17. try	27. some	37. remember	47. watch
8. battle	18. folks	28. middle	38. street	48. order
9. want	19. maybe	29. ask	39. rush	49. right
10. small	20. ill	30. enough	40. one	50. buy

Exercise seven

1. O	11. S	21. S	31. O	41. S	51. O
2. S	12. O	22. O	32. S	42. O	52. O
3. O	13. S	23. O	33. O	43. O	53. S
4. O	14. O	24. S	34. S	44. O	54. O
5. S	15. O	25. S	35. O	45. S	55. O
6. O	16. O	26. O	36. O	46. O	56. O
7. S	17. S	27. O	37. O	47. S	57. S
8. O	18. O	28. O	38. S	48. O	58. O
9. O	19. S	29. S	39. O	49. O	59. S
10. S	20. O	30. O	40. O	50. S	60. O

Exercise eight

1. c	10. b	19. a	28. a	37. a	46. b
2. d	11. b	20. d	29. c	38. c	47. c
3. a	12. c	21. d	30. b	39. c	48. b
4. c	13. b	22. b	31. d	40. b	49. c
5. b	14. a	23. c	32. d	41. d	50. c
6. c	15. d	24. d	33. b	42. b	
7. a	16. c	25. a	34. c	43. d	
8. d	17. b	26. b	35. b	44. d	
9. c	18. b	27. d	36. c	45. d	

Exercise nine

1. √	6. ○	11. ○	16. ○	21. √	26. √
2. ○	7. √	12. √	17. √	22. ○	27. ○
3. ○	8. ○	13. √	18. √	23. ○	28. √
4. √	9. √	14. √	19. √	24. √	29. √
5. ○	10. ○	15. ○	20. ○	25. ○	30. ○

Exercise ten

1. b	6. c
2. d	7. b
3. a	8. a
4. d	9. d
5. d	10. c

Exercise eleven

1. c	6. c	11. a	16. b
2. b	7. b	12. d	17. b
3. b	8. a	13. d	18. d
4. d	9. c	14. a	19. a
5. d	10. b	15. c	20. c

Exercise twelve

1. c	6. b
2. b	7. d
3. a	8. c
4. b	9. b
5. d	10. a

Exercise thirteen

1. d	6. c
2. b	7. b
3. c	8. d
4. a	9. c
5. a	10. d

Exercise fourteen

1. b	6. d
2. c	7. b
3. c	8. a
4. b	9. d
5. c	10. a

Exercise fifteen

1. e	6. b
2. c	7. a
3. d	8. e
4. a	9. b
5. d	10. c

Exercise sixteen

The following words should be underlined:

1. one	6. grants of land
2. Columbia University	7. 13
3. 182	8. the University of Maryland
4. St. Louis University	9. Newcomb College
5. a national university	10. Eight

Exercise seventeen

1. c	6. d	11. d	16. a
2. b	7. a	12. c	17. b
3. d	8. c	13. d	18. c
4. c	9. b	14. c	19. c
5. d	10. d	15. b	20. d

Exercise eighteen

part one		part two	
1. 906	11. 911	1. 1304	11. 1310
2. 914	12. 903	2. 1302	12. 1306
3. 909	13. 908	3. 1303	13. 1312
4. 903	14. 913	4. 1308	14. 1306
5. 912	15. 906	5. 1301	15. 1313
6. 901	16. 901	6. 1309	16. 1306
7. 900	17. 915	7. 1305	17. 1308
8. 914	18. 910	8. 1311	18. 1312
9. 900	19. 913	9. 1300	19. 1300
10. 907	20. 902	10. 1307	20. 1306

Reading-Time Conversion Table
for Exercises 2, 12, 13, 14

In the first column find the time it took you to read the selection, to the nearest fifteen seconds; in the second column find your reading rate in words per minute (WPM).

reading time	rate in WPM
1 min.	1000
1 min. 15 sec.	800
1 min. 30 sec.	667
1 min. 45 sec.	571
2 min.	500
2 min. 15 sec.	444
2 min. 30 sec.	400
2 min. 45 sec.	364
3 min.	333
3 min. 15 sec.	308
3 min. 30 sec.	286
3 min. 45 sec.	267
4 min.	250
4 min. 15 sec.	235
4 min. 30 sec.	222
4 min. 45 sec.	210
5 min.	200
5 min. 15 sec.	190
5 min. 30 sec.	182
5 min. 45 sec.	174
6 min.	167
6 min. 15 sec.	160
6 min. 30 sec.	154
6 min. 45 sec.	148
7 min.	143
7 min. 15 sec.	138

reading time	rate in WPM
7 min. 30 sec.	133
7 min. 45 sec.	129
8 min.	125
8 min. 15 sec.	121
8 min. 30 sec.	118
8 min. 45 sec.	114
9 min.	111
9 min. 15 sec.	108
9 min. 30 sec.	105
9 min. 45 sec.	103
10 min.	100